A BOY SURVIVES

A Journey through Polio with Hope, Self-Discovery, Healing, and Resilience

J. Benjamin Roe, Jr., D.MIN

A Boy Survives: A Journey through Polio, with Hope, Self-Discovery, Healing, and Resilience
Copyright © 2024 by J. Benjamin Roe, Jr., D.MIN

All rights reserved. No part of this publication may be reproduced or transmitted in any form or by any means, electronic or mechanical, including photocopy, recording, or any information storage and retrieval system without express permission in writing from the author.

Photo credits on page 171

Cataloging-in Publication Data
ISBN: 979-8-9877315-9-8

RC 180.1 B24 617.481 RO

J. Benjamin Roe, Jr.
Arvada, Colorado USA
ben@jbenjaminroe.com

Cover and Book Design Production by
Rebecca Byrd Arthur

Printed in the United States of America

Praise for *A Boy Survives*

How does one summarize a lifetime into a few words? Ben's autobiography is an in-depth discussion of the long-term impact on his life of his experience with polio at two and a half years of age.

Being a typically developing toddler in all areas of development and suddenly losing use of his body; being removed from family contact for three months; not having language to understand what was happening to him; and being handled by people who meant well, but had no idea of how to be with a toddler with serious illness all led to deep wounds that impacted his life.

Great read to help others understand the importance of the earliest years of development and how they impact us during our lifetime.

—Karla Stromberger, *retired pediatric physical therapist*

Ben's story shows what the human spirit can achieve. Surviving polio during a time when parents weren't allowed to see their kids in hospitals and disabilities weren't talked about, Ben shares openly about how this early-life trauma affected his heart and relationships — and how he healed. This is the story of how you survive when a terrible disease rips the bandaid off of your childhood.

—Jill Eelkema,
LCSW therapist and facilitator of post-polio support groups

Ben Roe has written a moving and vulnerable account of surviving and of thriving throughout his journey with polio as a child and as an adult. He shares his experiences of isolation, detachment from family, resilience, and great hope.

This is a deeply human story, and I came away with new insights and greater empathy about childhood trauma and family systems.

The book will be especially valuable for those in the post-polio community as well as nurses, chaplains, educators, and all caregivers.

—Rev. Dr. Harvey C Martz

*To Maggie
a blessing, best friend forever, and
key to my "earned attachment"*

Dance, when you're broken open.
Dance, if you've torn the bandage off.
Dance in the middle of the fighting.
Dance in your blood.
Dance when you're perfectly free.

    – Rumi (Persian poet and Sufi mystic born 1207)

Composer Anna Cline used this poem as inspiration for her composition "Dance," performed by the Colorado Symphony February 24, 2024, conducted by Conductor Laureate Marin Alsop, who was Music Director of the Colorado Symphony for 12 years.

Table of Contents

Note to My Readers xiii
Preface   *On Identity* xv
          What is Polio?.. xix
          Post-Polio Realities xx
          A Brief History of Methodism xxii

PART I: MY LIFE: A CHRONOLOGY 1
Introduction: CQ Transcendence 3

ONE   **Setting The Stage**..5
            Introducing My Family of Origin.............................5
            Early Years..13
            Polio: Childhood Upended....................................15
            My Journey with Polio..16

TWO   **School Years**..18
            Bayard: Discovering Nebraska 18
            Big Springs: Exploring Nebraska 20
            Ainsworth: Junior and Senior High Blossoming 27
            My Junior Year 30
            My Senior Year 32
            The Senior Prom 33
            Amateur Radio 34
            College: "Free at Last" 37
            Decision to Enter Ministry 43
            Seminary 46

THREE   **Ministry… and Burnout**...................................53

FOUR	The Lincoln Era 57
	Career Assessment and Recovery 58
	Community of Grace 62
FIVE	Denver: Go West! 66
	Warren Church 67
	Survival 70
	Back in the Church 74
	Activism 77
SIX	Our Move to Arvada 79

PART II: DIVING DEEPER 83	
SEVEN	Polio: My Personal Disaster 85
	Remembering and Assessing the Damage 86
	Family Complications and Healing 100
	Counseling and Therapy Experiences 107
EIGHT	Sexuality: The Puzzle 110
	Pleasure and/or Abuse? 110
	Why? 112
	Clarity 115
NINE	Ministry in Human Sexuality 119
	My Decision to Leave MHS 125
TEN	The United Methodist Debate 128
ELEVEN	Friendship, Love, and Marriage 134
TWELVE	Music and Its Place in My Life 143
THIRTEEN	Travel Highlights 149
FOURTEEN	Concluding Thoughts 159

PART III: ADDENDA 165

Images/Captions for *A Boy Survives* 167

Photo credits/permissions 171

Annotated Bibliography 173

Appendix A: Meditation on Disability and
        Body Image 181

Appendix B: Coming Out as a Bi Believer 183

Appendix C: What Do We Know About Sexuality? 187

Appendix D: A Word About My Faith
        Commitments 189

Appendix E: Phyllis Carol Roe: Wounded Healer 191

Acknowledgments and Gratitudes 195

About the Author 197

Note to My Readers

I've written this story of my life mostly for myself, to make sense of my journey, and to develop a "coherent narrative" of my life and experience, as Daniel Siegel urges in his book *Mindsight*, defining "coherent narratives" as "the way we make sense of our lives and free ourselves from the prisons of the past." (Siegel, 2010, 70) This is so important, he repeats later: "Making sense is a source of strength and resilience…I've also come to believe that making sense is essential to our well-being and happiness." (173)

I have also written it for anyone who is curious about how I came to be the person you know or may have met. I feel good about the progress I've made, and I look forward to more development and more growth.

Finally, I have written this for anyone who cares about what happens to young children and the burdens they carry from trauma and other "adverse childhood experiences." My story is about me as a young child who set about trying to "figure things out" mostly on my own and the discoveries and decisions I made over the next seven decades. The experience of polio at 29 months was a disaster for me as this child; and, because of hospital rules in 1948 and an early sexual experience, I was set up to solve two puzzles: sexuality, and the origin of pervasive sadness and loneliness. These are explored in some depth in Part II, after the basic chronology and stories of my life. The psychological concept of "attachment" is critical in understanding what happened to me. Facing the consequences of the "insecure attachment" that happens under these circumstances is what has helped me write this story. Readers who have been traumatized by abandonment and/or sexual abuse as a child should know that these issues are discussed frankly in Part II.

I think about the trauma of the children separated from their parents at the southern border of the USA and those who lose parents in war, and my heart is heavy because the recovery from their trauma will likely last a lifetime.

Throughout this piece, I will be mentioning various books and authors whose writings have been influential and helpful in my journey of life and understanding it. I have provided a bibliography at the end, which further documents the sources of these helpful concepts and ideas. Also, in the appendices are several things I've written which might be helpful.

I will be breaking one of the rules of my family of origin: never talk about the family outside the family. I will try to be graceful, truthful, respectful, and careful in what I say about things that happened in the parsonages in which I grew up. Nevertheless, I pray for your understanding of these basic truths: no pastor, and no pastor's family is perfect, without stresses and troubles. That goes for nearly every family, I know. Remember, too, that every parent of children born early in a marriage is still growing up, and brings the patterns of their own families into the home, because that is what they learned, for better and for worse. So much of what I say here is due to these two truths. Finally, we all live in societies that are also not perfect and have patterns learned over millennia. Sometimes societies regress and sometimes they progress. What counts as either is subject to great debate in some cases and barely aware in others. My story is just my story, and other members of my family, whether already "graduated" into the great beyond or aging as I am, will have different experiences of the same family from their own experience and perspective along with their own gifts, graces, and limitations. If others outside my family are mentioned, some names and some details have been changed to protect their identity.

PREFACE

On Identity

Who am I? Who have I been? What meaning has my life had? I've had these kinds of questions most of my life, and this section lays out some of the ways I've reflected on them. In this story of my life, I lay out experiences that have led to these questions. At the very least, this writing is my attempt to make some sense out of the various strands of my life experience, weave them into a meaningful pattern, and hopefully do it in an interesting way. And at best, my experiences and my reflections on them may be useful and maybe even helpful to others in their life journeys. In philosophical language, this is at least in part an exercise in "critical self-transcendence," as theologian and ethicist Reinhold Niebuhr insisted was what makes us human in his two volumes, *The Nature and Destiny of Man* (1941).

The experiences I've had and the choices I've made have shaped and in a sense have made me who I am. My life is thus a confluence of these experiences and decisions and what I've been able to weave into something meaningful. Most of these experiences are laid out in the first part of this story in the form of a chronology of stories. The most critical of them are explored in some depth in part II, "Diving Deeper." An overview of what I've learned and "figured out" is mostly in the Concluding Thoughts section at the end, but some conclusions I've come to are also throughout this narrative, as well as how I arrived at them. The early event of contracting the viral disease of polio and childhood experiences in my family were critical in how I went about my life after that event. The full impact of that experience has only recently become much clearer. But these early experiences set up my questions of identity and led to the biggest puzzle of my life: sexuality, which is explored in some detail in major sections after the basic chronology of my life is outlined.

What's in a life? Is a life a series of discrete events strung along an imaginary timeline from birth to death, or a line from the relationship of parents to the legacy of memories of others and impacts on the world around? What is that which holds a life together? Is it a stream of consciousness throughout one's years? Is it "the self," perhaps? If it's a "self," what about the things that happen before a "self" is formed, while the self is coming together and development is taking place, as philosophers, psychiatrists, and psychologists like Masterson, Erickson, Maslow, Piaget, Kohlberg, Fowler, Wilber, and others work to discover, theorize, categorize, and explain? Is a life actually a series of choices made by something in a person that actually makes choices?

Here are some of the roles and positions I've held during my years as a living human being: student, teacher, leader, pastor, minister, pastoral counselor, sex educator, organizer of advocacy events, radio announcer and engineer, cable TV broadcast engineer, videotape editor, secretary and office assistant, customer service tech, Unix applications programmer and trainer, webmaster, committee chair, communications staffer, board member…

How should I characterize this series of roles, positions, skills, knowledge sets? When I'm asked what I did before I retired (and just when did I actually retire?), I usually choose several of these depending on who's asking.

But which am I? Am I one or more of them? Is my identity a role, position, set of beliefs, values, and commitments? What might be an overarching theme that ties all of it together? You, my reader, will probably have a better sense of this as you read.

"You get to choose," my spouse Maggie and I remind each other. I'm free to make decisions about who I am, to decide to do or be this or that, to put energy into this and not that. "You are free to choose." But what is the "you" being referred to? Am "I" the overarching thread of consciousness that experienced all these things and many others? "A renaissance man" is how my spouse describes me. I sometimes say I'm a jack of all trades and master of none. Good at a variety of things, but not truly a master of any of them. The remainder of this piece lays out the various choices I've made along the way of my experiences and my best understanding of why I made them, and how they shaped me.

I think most folks in my generation, born in the 1940s and early 50s, grew up thinking one's vocation was something one discovered and then followed. A "calling," perhaps. Like it came from outside of oneself. That's the way ministry is often talked about. But is that my experience? Was I ever "called"? Is a calling something other than a religious experience? I like the way theologian Frederick Buechner put it: "The place God calls you to is the place where your deep gladness and the world's deep hunger meet" (1993, 119). Hearing this the first time was a revelation. In light of this, many times, I think I've (roughly) been following my "call" as best I have been able.

A story sometimes attributed to the writer Kurt Vonnegut resonates very much with me about this issue of "the call." He writes about working on an archeological dig as a fifteen-year-old. He says he was talking to one of the archeologists who was asking those kinds of "getting to know you" questions you ask young people: questions about sports, favorite subjects, and so on. The young man answered, "No, I don't play any sports. I do theater, I'm in choir, I play the violin and piano, I used to take art classes." The archeologist replied, "WOW. That's amazing!" In response, Vonnegut said, "...but I'm not any good at ANY of them."

The next thing the scientist said was what resonated with me as well as with the writer: "I don't think being good at things is the point of doing them. I think you've got all these wonderful experiences with different skills, and that all teaches you things and makes you an interesting person, no matter how well you do them."

I've wondered sometimes, like the writer, whether I've been something of a failure because I've had so many interests and yet haven't felt like I've excelled at them. "Don't spread yourself too thin" was one message I got as a teenager, and "You're not applying yourself."

In most of the work experiences, hobbies, and roles I write about in this piece, I've enjoyed something—often much—about each one. Each one has resonated with me in a significant way.

But behind all the varied experiences I've had and the questions of my vocation or calling is the question of identity. The source of this issue will become clearer, perhaps, as I describe my life and reflect on my experiences. One statement about this identity question that has meant a lot to me comes from Lutheran pastor Dietrich Bonhoeffer in this meditation from his Nazi prison cell.

WHO AM I?

Who am I? They often tell me
I stepped from my cell's confinement
Calmly, cheerfully, firmly,
Like a squire from his country-house.
Who am I? They often tell me
I used to speak to my warders
Freely and friendly and clearly,
As though it were mine to command.
Who am I? They also tell me
I bore the days of misfortune
Equably, smilingly, proudly,
Like one accustomed to win.
Am I then really that which other men tell of?

Or am I only what I myself know of myself?
Restless and longing and sick, like a bird in a cage,
Struggling for breath, as though hands were compressing my throat,
Yearning for colors, for flowers, for the voices of birds,
Thirsting for words of kindness, for neighbourliness,
Tossing in expectations of great events,
Powerlessly trembling for friends at an infinite distance,
Weary and empty at praying, at thinking, at making,
Faint, and ready to say farewell to it all.

Who am I? This or the Other?
Am I one person to-day and to-morrow another?
Am I both at once? A hypocrite before others,
And before myself a contemptible woebegone weakling?
Or is something within me still like a beaten army,
Fleeing in disorder from victory already achieved?

Who am I? They mock me, these lonely questions of mine.
Whoever I am, Thou knowest, O God, I am thine!
                              (Bonhoeffer, 1962, 221)

That such an esteemed theologian as Bonhoeffer could write this has been a comfort to me. In this story of my life, I will be writing about the events and decisions that could be called my life, the journey of my soul, the rooms of my "castle." These kinds of questions continue to puzzle me, even while writing this piece! More work to be done, I know. My best answers to date will be summarized at the very end.

What is Polio?
I had polio when I was two years old, and this is a critical part of my story. The details appear in the extended sections dealing with the disaster that polio was for a two-year-old. The

word "polio" is a short form of "poliomyelitis," a viral disease spread through fecal material to the digestive tract (my toddler explanation for how I got it was, "I ate dirt." Not so far off, huh?). Only a very small percentage of people who get infected by the polio virus develop paralytic polio, and of those, a small percentage develop "bulbar polio," the kind that infects the bulbar part of the spinal column that directs breathing (thus needing assistance like an "iron lung") and even swallowing. In paralytic polio, the virus attacks and somewhat randomly kills anterior horn cells in the spinal column, the cells that, through long fibers, connect to the muscle cells that produce movement. My type was, thankfully, not bulbar, but it did affect my upper left arm triceps, left chest pectoral muscles, right hip and quadriceps muscles, right calf, ankle, and foot muscles. The rehab process is often lengthy, at first focused on easing the painful contractions of early infection (thus, the Sister Kinney treatments and warm therapeutic tanks of water) and then over the next several years, encouraging the surviving anterior horn cells to sprout to cover more muscle cells, thus producing larger muscle motor units. Orthopedic surgeries can alleviate things like, in my case, different leg lengths due to the lack of muscle tension on the bones, and floppy feet like my right one. Thankfully, the polio vaccines introduced in 1955 and 1961 have nearly eradicated this awful disease worldwide.

Post-Polio Realities

Polio often has life-long effects, some of which remain stable after maximum recovery but for others the effects become progressive. Some survivors have permanent paralysis, which means that some specific and random muscles don't get messages from the brain to contract, and so atrophy from disuse. The progressive "late effects" form a syndrome called post-polio, or PPS. In my case, symptoms of PPS began to show in the early 1990s.

These late effects of polio may show up some 20 to 40 years later. In my case, over forty years after I had the acute stage of polio, I began developing new weakness and pain, usually through what is called "over-use." This means surviving nerve cells supplying the muscles with their instructions experience overloading and die off, producing new weakness. The orphaned muscles atrophy from disuse and shrink. My experience with this disease and its aftereffects forms a major part of my story, physically and psychologically.

The obvious presenting factor in my case for these symptoms showing up in the early 1990s was my decision to do most of the packing and moving (with some help from a friend who was stronger) during our relocation from Lincoln, Nebraska, to Denver, Colorado, via U-Haul in 1988. It was after work one evening in about 1991 that I hurt so bad I could hardly walk to my car to drive home. That was the stimulus for an evaluation at the Spalding Rehabilitation Clinic. I got a brace in 1991, and my first three-wheel mobility scooter in about 1992. I had probably five or six different scooters until a physical therapist in 2021 suggested a power wheelchair would be more appropriate. I've learned from reading some research and from my physical therapist that keeping active and doing limited exercise will help keep muscles that are left from atrophying. The key is to stop before significant fatigue sets in on the particular muscles in use. The risk is that over-stressing the nerve cells that supply the muscles will cause them to die, and new weakness follows. It's a maddening balancing act.

The Colorado Post-Polio organization has provided retreats and support groups, which help expand understanding and coping strategies. It helps when family members participate.

One characteristic of polio survivors is that we tend to be over-achievers, "type A" folks (Bruno, 2002, 98f). As my story unfolds, you can see elements of this characteristic. As I saw it at the time, I was just doing what I could to survive and "figure it all out myself" in a meaningful way. How this came to be and unfolded over my lifetime is a major theme in my story. In Chapter Seven, I share poems and stories which detail my journey of "figuring it out," of discovery of the depth of the psychological and emotional journey of my life.

A Brief History of Methodism

Methodism was founded by Church of England priest John Wesley. As a fellow at Oxford he formed a "Holy Club" which was so spiritually disciplined that they became known as "Methodists." It was a renewal movement of the Church of England, but because he wanted to preach to the common people, he was eventually not welcome as a preacher in the church. The folks who were attracted to Wesley's "way of holiness" in personal and social action formed small groups to help each other keep growing spiritually.

He and his brother Charles were the main leaders, Charles being a prolific hymn-writer. John was a prolific writer, expounding his views of the good news of God's grace above all. He visited the Americas and started gatherings in Georgia. In 1784, as the USA was coming into being, Methodists formally met in Baltimore to form the Methodist Episcopal Church, with a "Book of Discipline" to guide the new movement.

In 1844, the church split into northern and southern denominations: the Methodist Episcopal Church in the north, and the Methodist Episcopal Church, South, almost entirely in the south. The northerners were strongly against slavery, and the southerners strongly supported the institution of slavery. The Methodist Protestant Church was founded in 1828. These three branches were reunited in 1939 to form The Methodist Church. Then the Evangelical United Brethren and The Methodist Church united in 1968 to form The United Methodist Church.

In this book, when the word "Methodist" appears alone, it refers either to the denomination The Methodist Church (from 1939-1968) or to a generic Methodist-oriented idea or group. When referring to The United Methodist Church denomination (since 1968), the word United will be present. Much more is at this link (www.resourceumc.org/en/content/a-brief-history-of-the-people-of-the-united-methodist-church).

PART I
MY LIFE: A CHRONOLOGY

Introduction: CQ Transcendence

This phrase came from the introduction to a biographical statement I wrote for Clinical Pastoral Education (CPE) in 1987. I've been an amateur radio operator since eighth grade. "CQ" is amateur radio lingo for a "general call" to any station. "CQ Transcendence" roughly translated could be, "I seek you, Transcendence."

As I've said above, confusion and uncertainty about my identity have dogged me most of my life and have led me to an awareness of loneliness, sadness, and frustration, feelings that describe my childhood and adolescent years. Escape was my wish, and transcending through mind and spirit was my attempted method. As it turns out, I've since learned that facing these feelings directly is, in fact, the best way to ultimately transcend them!

Loneliness came partly because of my differences: physical limitations because of polio and frequent illness throughout childhood—and I was a preacher's kid, which, like kids of teachers, often sets one off from classmates. But the origin of the loneliness lies in my initial experience of polio.

Sadness came from sensitivity to the pains of the world and the contrast with the way things could be. I remember making a scrapbook of the Korean War and the Hungarian uprising in the 1950s. I was sad that the world was the way it was.

Family dynamics were an important factor, too, because of my distance from my dad and what I saw very early on as my mom's emotional issues. I was sad as well, as I could see that something was wrong at home. I would see the public image projected at church by both mom and dad, and hear the ruminations, criticisms, and paranoia of mom, dad's belittling criticism of her, and the bickering between both of them at home. I tried for years to change it. (I was never successful, of course, which contributed to the frustration.) At one point my mom said something like, "You just wait. You'll be just like us!" I said back as strongly as I could without yelling, "I will not!" That has been a commitment that has guided my participation in the 55-year marriage I've had the privilege to share with my wonderful spouse, Maggie. It took a lot of work in therapy, but we've broken the spell.

Frustration came from polio-related disability, illness, parental dynamics, my learned helplessness and powerlessness to change my family, the world, and my body.

So this story is about solving puzzles of my life: the pervasive loneliness and curiosity about sexuality.

ONE

Setting The Stage

Introducing My Family of Origin

Welcome to the Roe family: Joe, Enid, Ben, Phyllis, Rebecca, and Deborah. I'm grateful to have had the influence of each of them, and proud of each member in their unique ways: dad, for his strength of commitment to his ministry; mom for her sensitivity and service to the less privileged; both of them for treating their disabled kid "like any other child," and for their convictions; Phyllis, for her gift of pastoral counseling and spiritual wisdom; Rebecca, for her creativity, wit, and perseverance with a terminal illness; and Deborah for her creativity and care for her adopted family.

My father, Joseph Benjamin Roe, Sr., was a native of Arkansas, born in 1920 in Des Arc, Arkansas, on the White River, northeast of Little Rock. He was named after two grandfathers, Joseph Hartsoe and William Benjamin Roe.

My mother, Enid Adrian Talton, was born in 1921 in El Dorado, Arkansas, near the southern border with Louisiana. She grew up in Mansfield, near Fort Smith.

Dad and Mom were both members of the Methodist Episcopal Church, South, and met at Methodist-related Hendrix College in Conway, Arkansas, and were married August 31, 1942, in Texarkana, at the parsonage of the District Superintendent. (A District  Superintendent or D.S. is a supervisor of clergy and churches in an area called a district.)

Both Mom and Dad experienced the Depression, which made a lasting impression on them, and thus on the whole family, as money always felt very limited—and of course, a minister's salary was no great shakes, either.

Dad's dad, Thomas Gilbert, was an accountant in the hardware store in Des Arc. He died when dad was eleven. Dad's older brother, Thomas G., Jr. died at age 15 when my dad was ten. Dad's mom, Minnie, handled five kids from then on, and "took in laundry" as a way to make ends meet, I was told. Dad went to high school in Des Arc, and told a story about getting a cow up into the school belfry once. So while he was a serious young man headed for ministry, he could also be a prankster (a trait his daughter Rebecca picked up).

 Dad attended Garrett Biblical Institute in Evanston, Illinois (now Garrett-Evangelical Theological Seminary). This decision was politically a problem for him in the Little Rock Conference in those days because the preferred seminary was Perkins School of Theology in Dallas, affiliated with the ME Church, South. But, he wanted to study with faculty member Georgia Harkness because of her outspoken and prophetic words about racism, women's equality, and liberal theology and ethics. When I learned this in my teen years, I was proud of him for standing up for his convictions.

Dad started his ministry in the Little Rock Conference of The Methodist Church in the 1940s, serving "circuits" of several churches at which he would preach on Sundays and probably Wednesday nights in those days. "Circuits" meant that dad served at least two churches on each "circuit." This meant we lived in small towns in my early years.

Dad was a Methodist minister and then a United Methodist minister for nearly 40 years, serving in the Little Rock and Nebraska Conferences. (A "conference" is an organization of Methodist clergy and laity in a region and usually meets annually to handle regional church business.)

When we moved to Arkansas after dad graduated from Garrett, we landed in Tillar. Dad served the Tillar and then Strong "circuits."

Dad also served Methodist churches in Bayard, Big Springs, and Ainsworth, Nebraska, and United Methodist Churches in Elmwood, Lincoln, Shelton, and Arapahoe, Nebraska. He retired from Arapahoe, and he and mom moved to Norton, Kansas in 1985, where she continued to teach special ed until her retirement.

He was active in the church camping program in the Nebraska Conference, serving as director of several camps. He encouraged me to go to church camp nearly every summer, which was a formative set of experiences for me. He enjoyed tent camping with the family as well. We were still living in small towns in Nebraska when he was honored by the conference as Rural Pastor of the Year in 1964, the year I graduated from high school. I was proud of his recognition.

He was a woodworker, making furniture-like book cases and a step stool with big bunny ears for support. We called them "Bunny Steps." He made small wooden vehicles for me to play with, including a wooden open jeep and a garage of four trucks. My sister Phyllis and I used to play with these upstairs in the Bayard parsonage.

When I got interested in astronomy in later grade school he helped me build a four-inch reflecting telescope and built a simple but strong tripod for it. Later, when I got a different type of mount, he strengthened it with his carpentry skills. I found a design, and he built two large bass reflex speaker enclosures for me as a young adult. I recently had to replace the worn-out speakers, and had to figure out how to open the sturdy wooden boxes and reconfigure them for the new speakers. They still sound good.

He died from an aortic aneurysm in 1987. His death led me into a period of deep reflection and grief.

My mother Enid had wanted to be a missionary but (as she usually put it) married dad instead. Her dad was a supervisor of a brick plant in Mansfield. She was fourth out of five kids.

Mom was active in local church activities in the churches dad served, primarily with the Women's Society of Christian Service ("WSCS") and United Methodist Women. She was the family cook, and nearly always put either a chicken or meatloaf in the oven right before she went to church, which was usually next door. She baked things for the church bake sales and, later in life, became quite skilled at crafts, usually involving sewing.

After I left home for seminary, she finished a master's degree in education, begun in the 1940s at Northwestern and completed at the University of Nebraska in 1976, and began teaching special education. She became a diaconal minister in the United Methodist Church. (A diaconal minister is one of several types of ordained, consecrated, or approved ministers in the United Methodist Church.) She taught special education in Norton, Kansas, when dad was assigned to

Arapahoe, Nebraska. She was honored for her work in special ed by the school district. She was sensitive to the less fortunate and to justice and fairness issues, and more than once stood up for injustices either in the school or in society.

She experienced trauma as a girl. The Depression deeply marked folks who grew up in that era. Her family lost their house in town and car when she was about eight, when they moved to the brick plant. She lost an uncle to a car accident when she was nine. An alcoholic grandfather lived with them. Both grandparents died when she was in college, and her own father died two years later. All her life, she dealt with feelings of inferiority, I think partly at least in comparison with her more out-going older sister. An accident with scissors in her childhood that involved that sister left her without sight in one eye. She had difficulties with fully affirming the separate identities of her children, especially me. I had encouraged her over the years to seek therapy for her issues, which, as I reflected later on her symptoms and what I saw, included what I think must have been these traumas and abuse as a child, possibly sexual, and probably also corporal punishment as parental discipline, given the culture at the time regarding discipline of children.

My mom's death came in 2002 after her battle with non-Hodgkin's lymphoma. She underwent chemotherapy in Omaha several times in the late 1990s. As is often the case with chemotherapy, she lost her hair. When it came back in it was a gorgeous pure white. I think that at first, she didn't like it. (She'd colored her gray hair for years.) At the end of her life in 2002 in Norton, my spouse Maggie, my youngest sister Deb, and I spent a couple of weeks with her in home hospice care. I was sitting by her side and realized that she'd stopped breathing. I broke into tears, thinking to myself, "She never did it (do therapy)." In my head, I heard her voice as clear as a bell, saying, "I'm sorry." And I cried even more deeply. My mom's death had layers of meaning for me, including this grief, the grief of missing out on having a mom who encouraged individuation, and who was able to use the therapy offered to her at one point. And I recognized my grief at not being better able to understand and love her as she was.

My sister Phyllis Carol was born just up the road from Tillar, Arkansas, in Dumas, 17 months after my birth. We were close, and yet fought a lot as children. I was not nice at times, even biting her when we were toddlers, but we grew closer as we got older. We also played together in our younger years and were in similar activities in high school. There was competition between us at various times.

She graduated from Nebraska Wesleyan the same year as Maggie and me. When I went to the West Coast for seminary, she went to New York City and got an M.Div. degree from Union Theological Seminary in New York City. She was a trail-blazer: the first woman in the Parish Internship Program in Youngstown, Pennsylvania. Phyllis and I were ordained elder in the same ordination ceremony in 1976. She graduated from Candler School of Theology at Emory University with a Doctor of Sacred Theology. She and her classmates had t-shirts made with the line, "I got my STD at Emory." The degree was eventually retitled Doctor of Theology.

I greatly respected her career path: She was a pastoral counselor, a Fellow in the American Association of Pastoral Counselors (AAPC), and a leader in the Pacific Region of AAPC, as well as nationally. Phyllis served as Coordinator of Supervised

 Ministry and an Adjunct Professor at the Candler School of Theology. She was a counselor at the Georgia Association for Pastoral Counseling and co-authored the 1998 book *Reflections on Aging and Spiritual Growth*. She married Michael Anderson, who was a Ph.D. graduate and pastoral counselor from Emory. She and Michael were the first executive directors of the Samaritan Counseling Center of Hawai'i. I was proud of her for all these accomplishments, even as I felt a tinge of envy.

Phyllis's sudden, unexpected, and untimely death in 2001 hit us all very hard, in the family and well beyond it. She was undergoing surgery on an aortic aneurysm right at her heart, which made it a very difficult and specialized surgery. She experienced a lack of oxygen during surgery and ended up brain dead. Maggie and I traveled to New York City and gathered at her bedside in the hospital with her close friend Toni and the president of the AAPC who lived in the city. The shock was not only to her agency, Samaritan Counseling Center of Hawai'i, and to many in Hawaii where she was well-known, but to the entire AAPC organization where she was a respected leader.

Maggie and I traveled to Oahu and Honolulu for her memorial service and worked with the rest of the family and some close friends to handle her affairs. I was proud that my sister had developed a strong pastoral counseling presence not only for her clients, but also in the religious communities in Hawai'i as well as in the AAPC. My reflection during her memorial service is in an appendix and on my website, JBenjaminRoe.com. It was a very difficult time, and caused major strain on my relationship with my mother, given my distant relationship with the whole family.

In recognition of her influence, the AAPC put up a special page for remembrances by the many members who had been associated with and touched by her. I also have posted this page and much of her memorial service in Honolulu at First UMC.

My sister Rebecca was born in 1952 when I was six and we were living in Bayard, Nebraska. We were not particularly close, until I returned from seminary. She graduated from high school in Elmwood, Nebraska, and attended Nebraska Wesleyan University in Lincoln until she developed systemic lupus erythematosus (SLE), followed by kidney failure and dialysis. She was creative: she made banners and large macrame pieces and wrote poetry and prayers. A deeply meaningful banner she made spoke of her faith as a person who lived with the disability of SLE: "You can fly but that cocoon has to go." She died in 1978 from an aortic aneurysm and other complications of SLE. My sister Phyllis wrote about Rebecca, in a sermon and article in 1978. My sister Deb also wrote about Rebecca's "Prayer of Easter" poem. Her death was a turning point in my learning to deal with death. This death and the death of my sister Phyllis further impressed upon me the transitoriness of human life, and the gift of life that we have while we are living human beings.

My sister Deb was born in 1956, when we were living in Big Springs. Watching her struggle with mom's over-protectiveness helped me see more clearly some dimensions of my own family issues. She graduated from Lincoln Northeast High School and attended Kearney State College in Kearney, Nebraska, where she worked at a filter manufacturing company. Her dating a black man at one point caused huge problems for my mom.

She was an active science fiction fan and met her future husband, Dan Stratmann, at a St. Louis sci-fi convention. They were married on a memorable cold and sleety December day in St. Louis, where they started their life together. Dan studied at Eden Theological Seminary and became a UM minister (to her discomfort) in the United Methodist Missouri East Conference  and served churches in De Soto, Princeton/Mercer, and Pacific, before his sudden death from a pulmonary embolism in 2013. Deb appreciated Dan's creativity in his preaching. Her issue with the church is its very humanness: the criticisms she heard from church members, from mom of church members, and, of course the human politics of the institution. Deb worked for several years at Laclede Groves assisted living community as office manager for the chaplain, which included supporting a Clinical Pastoral Education program he supervised. Deb and Dan adopted Andrew Campbell of De Soto, who died in his sleep at the young age of 27, after finding his "ideal job." Deb then adopted Andrew's daughter Adriana, who is now a teenager. Deb and I weren't very close, mostly due to my own dynamics that are discussed elsewhere, but she has been an inspiration in her care for Adriana and in her interest in our family roots. Deb's creativity at making collages of photos is a gift, as seen in the ones she made of our sister Phyllis and of her own life.

Early Years

I entered this life and family in Illinois. Born in 1946 after over 13 hours of labor, I was the first child of Joe and Enid, who were living in a parsonage while my student pastor father finished his seminary education in Evanston. He was serving a

 student ministry charge in The Methodist Church in Montgomery, Illinois, near Aurora. I was born in a hospital in Aurora on April 12. I was baptized by Rev. Kermit Long on June 23, 1946, right before we moved back to Arkansas.

I was named after my dad: Joseph Benjamin Roe, Jr. The tradition in some parts of the country, especially southern society in those days, was to simply call the "Junior" member "Junior." But my parents wanted me to be known not just as "Junior," so they called me "Benny." My parents asked me what name I wanted on my first Bible, given by the church when I was in the third grade. I chose to have the name "Ben Roe" on it, nice, quick and easy, six letters, the first time I chose to be called "Ben"! I was growing up.

So, I was Ben Roe, or later J. Benjamin Roe until medical insurance, Social Security and the IRS insisted that I go by my full name. I now prefer J. Benjamin Roe, Jr.

When I was 10 months old, I began getting asthma attacks. Some were pretty serious and scary, not only for me but also for my parents. The image of the nebulizer used to treat my attacks is burned into my memory by the trauma of struggling to breathe. By the time I was four, my father put in for a transfer to a drier climate at the suggestion of our family doctor.

Mom and dad liked to read to us kids. Of course, we learned a lot about whatever they read to us, as well as the joy of reading! I enjoyed hearing about steam engines and listening to the radio next to my crib.

I liked to walk during these early years in Tillar. One day my mom took me to the grocery store with her. I got away from her and she couldn't find me anywhere in the store. When she went out the front door, she saw me sitting on the lap of one of the black men who were sitting in the front of the store, just talking away with him. It was probably one of my first experiences with a person of color. I have no memory of any significant reaction from my mom, other than undoubtedly an admonishment to stay closer to her.

Polio: Childhood Upended

I was 29 months old when disaster struck. I came down with polio. My polio experience had a crucial role in my development physically, emotionally, and psychologically at a critical time in my early life. This is the age when a toddler is refining their relationship with their parents and developing more independence, to put a complex concept simply.

At the time, we were living in Tillar, in southeast Arkansas, where dad served. My mother tells me that they first thought I had a cold. Then they began to be concerned when it looked like I was getting weaker and weaker. She told me I got so weak I could not lift my arms, legs, or head. My parents were probably extremely worried. They took me to the doctor several miles away in Dumas, who thought he recognized polio. He decided not to take time to confirm the diagnosis, and sent us on to the University Hospital in Little Rock, where all the polio cases were taken (there were 948 that year). The diagnosis was confirmed there on September 13, 1948. I was put in isolation in University Hospital for a month, so the disease could pass its communicable stage.

At the end of this period, I was transferred to Children's Hospital also in Little Rock, where I stayed another two months. Almost everything I know about the hospitals I was in for my earliest treatment comes from my mother. She told me parents could only visit their children an hour a week on Sundays, the day dad preached at least two times at towns a hundred miles away. I think I recall that she said that she and my father went to the hospital weekly on days other than Sundays, hoping to get to see me, but were always told they couldn't. When my father questioned this, he was told, "It makes the children easier to handle." When I first read this in a letter from my dad to his mom, I thought, "Yeah, it's like breaking their spirit"—which it nearly did to me. This experience and its consequences shaped my life profoundly, as I describe more fully in Part II. It would be almost 40 years before I was ready to explore the depths of those consequences.

My Journey With Polio

I came home at the end of the three months in the hospitals with a brace that went around my thigh, and all the way down my right leg, to a special shoe. Braces at that time were made of stainless steel, springs, and leather straps, attached to the shoes: heavy, cumbersome and off-putting to anyone who saw them. When I came back from the hospital in December, my family had moved to Strong, Arkansas, in south central Arkansas, near the border with Louisiana. I had a sand box and enjoyed spending time there. I'm sure that I was trying to process my experience while playing alone. I remember Strong was just putting in city water and had the road dug up in front of the parsonage. My first friend Tim lived across the street (and across the ditch for the water pipe). I liked him; we played together.

The long leg brace was reduced to a calf brace sometime around age four or five, I think. That brace was consigned to the trash when I was in second grade in Bayard. After we moved to Bayard, mom drove me to Scottsbluff for physical therapy weekly for months. And when the Salk vaccine was announced on my birthday in 1955, we lost no time in getting it! When Sabin introduced his vaccine in 1961, we took it too.

I had three orthopedic surgeries at Children's Hospital in Denver to help with the aftermath of polio, which had weakened my right leg, abdomen, and left upper chest and triceps.

The first surgery was done on my right ankle after we moved from Bayard to Big Springs, when I was about eight or nine. I think it was supposed to fix the drop foot issue, but it didn't accomplish that. When the casts came off after each surgery, I was terrified when I saw the saw that cut through the casts. I had not realized that the blade didn't turn: it vibrated back and forth. It would have been reassuring to have known that ahead of time. And the skin underneath was pretty gross, with the accumulation of around six or eight weeks of dead skin!

The second surgery was to the growth area of my left knee to slow down growth so my legs would be equal. But when the surgeon measured my leg bones after the cast came off, he got a puzzled look on his face: they weren't equal. But when he measured the length of my legs with me standing, from hip bone to floor, they were. This is because the two feet were very different: the right one was much thinner with no arch whatsoever, the left one thicker with a high arch. He—and we—were relieved.

The third surgery when I was 13 was to fuse the bones together in my right ankle, removing any ankle movement. This, of course, permanently fixed the droopy foot! It was the most painful of all the three surgeries. It has stayed solid all these years since, through the running, marching, and even falling I did as a teenager.

TWO

School Years

Bayard: Discovering Nebraska

As I mentioned, dad asked for a transfer to a drier climate because of my asthma. He applied to the Arizona and Nebraska Annual Conferences. Nebraska replied first, offering him a position in Bayard, in western Nebraska. We moved there in 1950. Mom told me that my asthma stopped as we crossed into Nebraska. We heard stories about the "blizzard of '49" which we just missed. These stories reminded us we were in a different climate! Sugar beets were the main crop, and there was a big sugar beet processing plant in town. For a time, mom worked the night shift there in food service.

Our move to Bayard from Arkansas was good for me. It lessened my asthma, and was an experience of expanding exploration. I learned to tie my own shoes around age five or so, and was so excited that I came downstairs when I was supposed to be napping to show mom. I often played with twin brothers from church, Jimmy and Timmy. There was an irrigation ditch running through town and when it was empty and muddy, we'd often explore the muck to find things that lived there. We would sometimes walk home from school and sometimes my friends would run ahead, leaving me behind, with me yelling, "Wait for me!" That wasn't a great feeling, and was something I wrote about in college freshman English class.

In kindergarten, I remember liking one girl a lot, but when I spent nearly half of the year in a hospital or at home with a "fever of unknown origin," I lost out with her and other experiences of kindergarten. Second grade in Bayard was especially lonely and painful, in part because of friction between the teacher and me. I think I was bored, and when I was caught doing something not related to the lesson, I was shamed in front of the whole class. I also had difficulties with peers on the playground. One experience I remember happened on the playground with a teeter-totter. I once sat on the pipe in the middle of it, and when one of the kids jumped off, the pipe came up and hit my mouth, cutting my lip and damaging a tooth. Luckily, my permanent teeth hadn't come in yet. Needless to say, I got a talking to and learned an important lesson about risk.

Phyllis and I used to climb on the apple trees in the backyard of the parsonage, and use them as a natural "jungle gym." She and I played upstairs in the parsonage with a little metal open-front playhouse, little rubber people, and  wooden vehicles my dad made. I once played inside a big pile of limbs that had been pruned, making my own little hiding place.

I remember the Sunday school gatherings, and especially liked the song "Fairest Lord Jesus." Still do, though the theology no longer matches mine.

I was a sensitive kid because of what I'd been through. I wondered about a lot of things, including Santa Claus, Jesus, war, and families. One thing I distinctly remember was that after learning that Santa Claus wasn't real, I seriously wondered if Jesus was real. I eventually worked this out by thinking about the millions of people over thousands of years who believed in his life and teachings, and I decided that this must mean he was real. (Much later, as a college student, I revisited this question by writing a paper on "The New Quest for the Historical Jesus," and concluded the same, this time based on a different kind of data!)

I should mention my experience with parental discipline, which I remember most strongly from this period. One way my parents disciplined us kids was using physical punishment. Discipline in the household was firm, but if I cried "too much," I might hear, "Stop crying or I'll give you something to cry about." Physical punishment was not common but it did happen: spanking with a hand most often, and with a switch (a small flexible branch from a bush: see Wikipedia) once by mom, and once with a belt by dad. I immediately felt the unfairness and abusive nature of this, but neither I nor my parents knew alternative punishments for whatever infraction I had done. "Minding" and "doing as you are told" were important rules in our household. I think these things were relatively common child-rearing practices in the 1940s and 50s. I'm glad that parents who want to can learn less abusive ways of guiding the behavior of children these days.

Big Springs: Exploring Nebraska

We moved from Bayard to Big Springs, Nebraska, the summer after my second-grade year. The years of third through sixth grade at Big Springs were the beginnings of feelings of greater capability. I did well in school without really working at it and was always nagged at "not living up to my potential." I enjoyed learning, though, and figured out from the results of an achievement test that I might have a high IQ. I decided I should keep this to myself. Expectations might get raised, you see, and I'd get hounded to perform more.

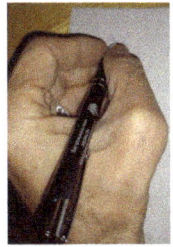

I learned to write cursive with my left hand, my natural preference, by watching the teacher's instructions and reversing them to fit my left hand. I have never written with the left-hand "hook" that seems to be common even today. (You can see "the hook" when some left-handers write, holding the pen so the left hand is held in a kind of hook, with the pen pointing away from the writer.)

I was running (awkwardly) in grade school, and in the kickball team choosing, I was always the last chosen, which was a bit painful, but I understood that running wasn't my strong suit. Kicking the ball wasn't either. Sometimes, my team would let a teammate do the base running for me.

I enjoyed singing and learning to play band instruments, such as snare drum, glockenspiel, and horn. In sixth grade, the marching band needed a drum major, and the band director chose to have me try it. It wasn't fun and didn't last long. The trombones were always pushing up behind me and using their slides to harass me! Instead, the band director decided it would be better for me to march with a drum or a horn. We worked out a plan to allow me to march in the parades we got to be in: I would be on the end of a row and would drop out somewhere along the route when I got tired. Marching band was torture, first with a snare drum bouncing on my leg, then with a French horn bouncing on my lips!

For five years in childhood, I had a cast on my right leg or my left one. Besides the surgeries, I somehow got a "greenstick" fracture of my right tibia. Then, my right kneecap was dislocated in some horsing around which I did with a friend one summer. I spent a lot of time in bed in my childhood. Besides the surgeries and accidents mentioned above, I dealt with asthma, with periodic attacks that usually came with a cold. I loved reading, and especially the little orange biographies ("Childhood of Famous Americans" series created by the Bobbs-Merrill Co.) from the Big Springs Library, just a few blocks from our house. I read most of them, and was inspired by the stories. I think I realized they were "fictionalized," but nonetheless they were interesting and meaningful to me as a child. I think these not only inspired me, but also encouraged my interest in history, which continues with me today.

As I lay in bed from the various illnesses and operations I had, I would watch the birds outside the window of my bedroom at the back of the parsonage. There was a bowl of water underneath the big tree next to the house in which they'd splash when it was hot. My mom was always glad that I could "entertain myself." My dad helped me build a crystal radio set hooked up to the end of a long wire out to the chicken coop. I never heard the 500 watt station KOGA in Ogallala, or anything else on it! But when the antenna was hooked up to a regular radio, it could pick up stations much further away.

Tent camping was something dad in particular enjoyed. He took us camping nearly every summer when we lived in Bayard and Big Springs in western Nebraska. We alternated between the Black Hills in South Dakota and Longs Peak in Rocky Mountain National Park in Colorado. I enjoyed watching him build campfires and helped put up the army surplus five-person tent, with cots, sleeping bags and blankets. I learned what it meant to be detailed and thorough. We once camped overnight in Torrington, Wyoming, and in the middle of the night we were hassled and apparently threatened by some loud guys and told to get out. We left in a hurry.

Getting the tent up was a major project, it seemed to me as a kid. The end poles were taller than I was, and the rolled up tent felt heavier than me, too. I helped get the stakes out, putting one at all the places they would be needed to anchor either the bottom of the tent walls or the ropes that held the tent roof out (and the tent upright!). I would hold the poles while dad would pound the stakes in, and then watch as he adjusted the tension of the ropes to get the right slope and tension on the tent roof. In the last couple of times out, I also got to help with these tasks.

We would carry water from the central pump to our table. In the early years, we would heat the water for washing off over the campfire. Later, we would heat it over the Coleman stove we had by then. We never got a shower put together, even though I had plans in one of my books. I often thought it would be a nifty addition to our camping life.

It took me several summers, and some maturing, to venture off by myself. One time was fun, when I climbed far up on a pine-covered hill and sat and just thought, enjoying the perspective and beauty. I remember reflecting on the size of this huge rock I sat on. It was bigger than I was, and it was not going to move anywhere!

I remember another time in particular when I went off by myself. We had camped near a small lake made by beavers, in a place between two tall peaks. I remember going to sit at the edge of the water and marveling at the beauty, calm, and peacefulness. I didn't have words for it at the time, but that place will always be in my mind as a place I can go to be near to the peacefulness of God, as God must have meant for us all to experience.

This spiritual journey continued as I was confirmed in The Methodist Church in sixth grade. Dad taught the membership class. I'm sure I was not a model student, but I never doubted that membership was something I wanted.

Big Springs was a time of branching out and exploring the world: I got a bicycle and a telescope and developed friends in the neighborhood. I was a Cub Scout, and I see in my Cub Scout book that I had made plans to build a simple two-tube radio, but never did it. I had progressed to Webelos rank right before we moved away.

I got the bike in fourth or fifth grade. Dad told me that a woman active in the Women's Society of Christian Service in Ogallala had a bicycle she was willing to sell to me. I needed to come up with two dollars, and it was mine. I saved my allowance and bought it. I watched dad take the bearings apart and clean and grease them. He worked on tightening the spokes and making the wheels "true." I took the fenders and the metal "gas tank" in the middle off and painted everything, a combination of red and white. I learned to ride without too much difficulty, though there were the usual scrapes and torn jeans from sliding in the gravel from a too-quickly-taken curve. The bike was a way for me to get away and try out my own independence and competence at a skill. I rode it to school daily.

My friend TJ lived nearby. He and I would ride all over town, and often south of town to the South Platte River. We explored, occasionally raced, though I doubt I ever won (with my weak right leg, I was never able to stand up and "pump"). We spent a lot of time together, exploring the South Platte River and the surrounding area on our bikes. We would occasionally get under a railroad trestle and experience the roar of a train over our heads! I enjoyed his companionship very much, even though we had significant differences in interests, social class, and religion. After we moved to Ainsworth, however, I didn't keep in touch with him and also didn't develop any friendships like that for years. I think this was because I had begun to be aware of my desire for a more physical relationship with boys, something that was not OK. I say more about this issue below.

A Boy Survives

For Christmas one year, I got a couple of "saddle bags" for my bike in which to take my stuff to school. Unfortunately, one morning I discovered someone had urinated in them. I never felt comfortable using them after that, partly because of the smell, and partly because it meant that someone probably "didn't like me." It was a difficult experience, and I interpreted it as just another example of how I couldn't fit into the community as a P.K. (preacher's kid).

Big Springs was a small town of 500 or so, with few street lights and really dark skies. I was enthralled with the night sky and built the four-inch reflector telescope from a kit I bought from Edmund Scientific. Dad built a simple but strong tripod, and eventually, I got a better tripod that he strengthened. I was amazed at the detail I could see on the moon. I kept a few weeks of hand-drawn images of the position of Jupiter's main four moons and got glimpses of other wonders such as Orion's M42 and Lyra's Ring nebulae. I developed my knowledge enough that I was able to give a night tour at one of the church camps I attended during the summers after sixth, seventh, and eighth grades.

Technology has been a fascination of mine from early on. My mom told me I had memorized the parts of a steam engine as a young child. I vaguely remember that I stuck a bobby pin in a wall socket when I was probably one or two. This blew the fuse with a huge bang, of course, and burned my fingers. I learned about the power of electrical current! I was also told that I put a screwdriver through the speaker of my parents' radio before I was two. I remember being fascinated by my uncle's radio outside of its case, with its glowing tubes and tuning capacitor showing.

In fifth and sixth grade, I found old radios in a pile of junk that was in the backyard of a friend's house. I took parts out of the junked chassis, and then took them apart: paper capacitors were discovered to be made out of several feet of narrow foil and waxed paper all rolled up together and connected to wires. Tubes were made of very fragile metal wires, plates, and filaments, all contained inside glass bulbs, and smelled awful when they were broken by a hammer. Even the metal ones were made like the glass ones, once you got the metal cover off—no small task. Then there were the magical coils, especially the ones in the shortwave radios: here was the key, along with the delicate tuning capacitor, to the selection of stations that were from far-off exotic places that helped me transcend where I was. Who knew that someday I would know how to actually talk to far-off places using amateur radio?

I used to spend hours trying to figure out how these old radios worked, before I knew of books that could begin to tell me in a way I could understand. I knew what was inside the metal cans, how the speakers were made, and the various ways the knobs were kept on their shafts.

I used to wish I could make them run but knew I couldn't because of my age and lack of knowledge. The kind of powerlessness I felt to make them run was parallel to the kind of powerlessness I felt to make myself run very far, the weakness and impotence to change some of the aspects of my young life that I wanted to change.

As I grew older, though, after we moved to Ainsworth, I did learn how to make them run. I learned to solder, read schematic diagrams, find parts wherever possible, and troubleshoot! My dad bought me an Army manual on vacuum tubes, which was very technical, but I found it very interesting, instructive and useful. I found I could use the amplifiers and speakers of the old radios to wire up the parsonage for intercoms and music. During junior high, my father found an article on converting an older, big-tube radio to the newer, smaller "miniature" tubes. I decided to try it. I got an older radio from the TV shop in town and rebuilt it like the article showed. When I finished it, I discovered it would tune shortwave frequencies (why that worked, I'm unsure). My shortwave listening hobby had begun. Shortwave listening is focused on listening to international broadcasters that use frequencies that are much higher frequencies than standard AM radio, and which can travel much longer distances. I spent hours listening to Radio Moscow, Radio Nederland, and HCJB in Quito, Ecuador. I had great fun with all that, and kept a log for several months before I got turned on to ham radio. Around 2010, I was given a communications receiver that I had drooled over in the seventies, complete with the previous owner's shortwave listener log! I was a regular listener to the BBC, now on public radio stations in Colorado. I was disappointed when they discontinued their shortwave service to North America, but the signal is, of course, pristine on local FM! Occasionally I listened to Radio Netherlands (now discontinued, too), China Radio International, and Radio Australia. I have also heard Radio Sweden in a short broadcast to North America. As I mentioned, hearing those stations so far away helped me keep perspective on my limited youthful existence, and helped me keep faith that a better life was possible.

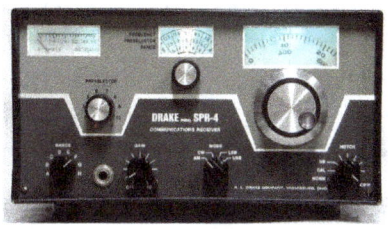

I have had dreams that included old radios and my desire to understand and make them work. I think old radios came to symbolize my sense of my power, the sound of a distant drummer, and my search for the source of my own life.

Ainsworth: Junior and Senior High Blossoming

We moved from Big Springs to Ainsworth, in northeast Nebraska, in the summer of 1958. One interesting issue with this move was a conversation I had with my dad when he was offered the position. He called me into his office in the Big

Springs church and told me about the offer. To my surprise, he then asked me what I thought! I said I thought it'd be a good thing: the town was bigger, the church was a bit bigger, as I recall, and they wanted him to help them build a new church. I was honored to be asked my opinion.

Ainsworth Junior High was a big change from Big Springs sixth grade! It was a larger school system, and it was a painful adjustment. I was in tears occasionally in the first six-week period because I experienced the material as hard and got lower grades on my first report card than I was used to. But by the end of the second six-week period, I had gotten into the swing of things and had brought my grades up to all As. Band was a saving grace because I found I could play the horn well.

Music became even more important, as I further developed my sense of individuality and skill by singing in choir and playing in band, continuing what I had started in Big Springs. During these years, my ability on the horn increased as I played first chair for several years, played in music contests and got good reports. One pivotal experience for me was a contest appearance as a junior. I had just finished playing, and walked back to where mom and dad were. Mom's first comment was something like, "Didn't you have your hand in the bell too far?" I decided I couldn't please her no matter how hard I tried. As important as that realization was, of course, it wasn't the end of that issue.

My first paying job ever was as a janitor at Ainsworth Methodist Church, mowing the lawn and getting up early on Sunday morning to turn on the heat for the church. That furnace was huge: a million Btu, as I recall, making an awesome flame in a large fire chamber and a great big old wooden blower (driven by a huge motor and multiple rubber belts!). It heated the whole church, including the sanctuary and education classrooms.

My next job was as a "soda jerk" with Morrow's Drive-in there in Ainsworth. I enjoyed working with other young people and making malts, shakes, cones, hamburgers, and fries. I think I may have gotten 50 cents an hour!

Several high school teachers were significant: they took me seriously, encouraged me, and challenged my development and competence. The teachers in math, English, science, and band were particularly influential. One English teacher was young and cute; I developed a crush on her. Another English teacher wasn't so nice: he assigned us a major research paper, and when we were to get them back, he told us he'd destroyed them so some other student wouldn't copy them! I had spent hours researching the history of the "French horn" and was proud of my work—he even gave me an A, I think. I was devastated, and got so angry that I was given detention (as I think I remember). I have rarely been that angry. I always kept a copy of my papers from then on. (So, I have quite a collection now!)

I loved arithmetic and English classes, and in high school, I liked algebra, and even geometry. Trigonometry wasn't too bad, either. I enjoyed physics in my later years and took a couple of science projects to science fairs in South Dakota. One was the radio I mentioned before, and the other was a small accessory box for my ham radio receiver. Neither got any particular recognition, but I had fun doing them, attending the fairs, and seeing what other kids had submitted.

I was into nearly everything in high school: band, chorus, class plays (*Arsenic and Old Lace* was one), student council. Our band even traveled to Miami and marched in the Orange Bowl Parade! I was involved in musicals (*Oklahoma!*, *South Pacific*, and *Annie Get Your Gun*). I remember that dad got involved briefly in a controversy over one of the songs in one of these, and I'm pretty sure he was on the more progressive side. I was the student manager for the sports teams. I even developed my writing skills as I wrote about high school sports for the town newspaper. I was active in Methodist Youth Fellowship in high school, locally and at the district level. I kept my interest in astronomy and increased my interest and activity in radio.

As I explore later, my strategy to survive and deal with the tensions and discomfort at home was to "keep busy" and learn and accomplish much. I realized at some level that I wasn't ready either emotionally or intellectually to deal with all that had happened in my earlier life. However, I also think that a good part of this "keep busy" agenda was trying out my various interests, skills, and leadership, and becoming more my own independent person.

My Junior Year

A Christian Citizenship Seminar around this time took me to New York and Washington, my first travel alone. It was fun riding in the front seat on the upper deck of the big Greyhound bus, especially when we ran into a big snowstorm coming into Chicago. It was a good learning experience. One highlight besides going to the UN was watching a black and white film called "Overture" which used Beethoven's "Egmont Overture" as the soundtrack to pictures of the state of the world, in poverty and war. I was in tears. That piece still brings me to tears. It was also good to be away from home and it helped me to distance myself just a little more from the parental apron-strings.

My high school junior class was responsible for putting on the junior-senior prom for the seniors. I was on the planning committee and remember some of the discussion of what we wanted to do. We wanted our prom to be different from all the others, and to be remembered. We planned a fountain:

someone had a small pump and knew how to hook it up so it would run. We wanted to do the ceiling differently, too. The tradition of a suspended ceiling of crepe paper strips was useful in turning the old town hall gymnasium/auditorium into a romantic environment. So what, besides colors, could be different? There were several rancher's kids on the committee. Someone remembered the old hay-rake wheels and axle sitting unused on their place, and suggested using it upended as a center support for a suspended ceiling that radiated out from it like many spokes on a wheel. We used the theme "Fantasy in Red." It was striking. My date to this event was probably the first-ever real "date" I had.

The summer after my sophomore year I had attended camp at the Methodist Camp Fontanelle near Fremont, and met a girl from a small town in northeast Nebraska. I fell in love. We kept in touch after camp, and so I invited her to the junior-senior prom. She accepted! Her town was over 70 miles away, and she was a sophomore. By now I was 16 and had my driver's license, so I drove to pick her up. Arrangements were made for her to stay over at a friend's home.

I don't remember much about the evening itself. I remember being proud of her and me for being there and being together. I remember most of all, though, the excruciating discomfort of not knowing what to do! I fell all over myself, as I remember it, to do everything just right, to put my wants and desires aside and minister to her every need. Well, I felt odd and strange about this—I knew that was what I was supposed to do, from all I had been taught about how one was supposed to treat girls. Mind you, I didn't really feel it was honest, just that was what I was supposed to do! But she got a little impatient with me because I hadn't thought much about what I wanted to do! It was the last time I tried so hard to play strictly by the book—someone else's book. It wasn't real, I didn't enjoy myself, and I don't think she did fully, either. I learned something about relating to others: be real. (Tall order, coming out of my family system, and one that would take some time to meet.)

My Senior Year

My senior year was a year of personal blossoming in some ways for me. I was in the senior class play, continued in band, musicals, National Honor Society, Blue Key, and other activities. I ran for student body president or vice-president. My slogan was "Roe, Roe, Roe Your Vote!" I don't remember that I was successful, but I did serve on the student council. I even went to Cornhusker Boys State.

One example of how this was a time of flowering for me was some of the activities that happened around the senior class play. One rehearsal, I and another cast member, a girl to whom I had been attracted for some time, went off during a long break to explore the steam tunnel between the older high school building and the newer grade school. I remember wanting to hug her and "get physical" as the song puts it today, but I didn't have the nerve to ask her, or to make a move nonverbally! It was still fun to be somewhere we weren't supposed to be. (This was quite against my image in those days, too.)

Then there was one night after rehearsal when I got the family car, took dad's two-gallon weed sprayer, rinsed it out good, filled it with water, and went out looking for the carload of senior girls who were driving around town. I had adjusted it to a long stream, so it was quite a water gun! I had fun that night!

Both of these incidents look like activities that don't seem particularly unusual, but for me, they marked a kind of beginning liberation of my own sense of self, a breaking out of my shell of studious, aloof but friendly preacher's kid and loner, to be more active with my classmates.

As I mentioned in the Preface on identity, now in high school, I worked on trying out and being involved in many activities, rather than focusing on and mastering just one. My senior class yearbook lists these activities: thespians, band, chorus, football student manager, class officer, student council, class play, honor society, newsletter staff, science club, county government day. Though I enjoyed something about each of these things, I was unsure about who I was and where I was going, and even how to decide!

Another experience of expanding my individuality and learning about the world outside my family and small town was my work during three summers in high school and early college, when I worked for the Nebraska Department of Roads. I was a traffic flagger ("flagman") with a maintenance crew and a striping crew, and a materials tester at a road paving construction site. These were interesting times with adult coworkers—and drivers! I learned some about the science of blacktop paving and about being more independent (what to choose to cook for supper, even!).

The Senior Prom

I did not go to my senior prom my last year of high school. The unpleasant memory of why resurfaced as I was leading a group of senior high students some years ago in a discussion of the question, "Should girls ask guys out?" Nearly all there agreed yes, but one male wondered how to say "no." I doubt I shared this story.

This experience is one of the more painful experiences of my senior year.

I had a reputation all through junior and senior high of being "nice." I took pains never to show anger (I seldom got angry anyway), always being conciliatory, friendly and helpful—and alone. I also seemed to be somewhat unusual among males in trying to treat girls as equals, not as objects. So it was a pretty safe bet that I would say yes if a girl asked me out. I wasn't dating anyone, either. So my classmate Jen asked me to the prom. She was active in her church (not Methodist) and in pep club. She had the misfortune not to know I did not find her attractive, and that I had had an awakening of a new sense of self-assertion. I struggled between wanting to be "nice" and wanting to go with someone else, between my old self and my emerging one. I said no (I'm sure it was quite awkward). I didn't go to the prom at all, in part not to compound the hurt. And I felt guilty because I had hurt her. It was also a clash of values between not hurting anyone, honoring a woman's place to be assertive, and my own personal agency to make my own decisions based on my preferences.

Amateur Radio

It was in Ainsworth where I was exposed to amateur radio. It was the summer of 1959, between the seventh and eighth grades. I was 13. That summer was my last and most painful polio corrective surgery. It was the occasion for further exploration of my interest in radio. I was listening to the radio a lot, and one summer day, I was listening, wanting to be outside in the sunlight instead of in bed with this cast on my right ankle.

Suddenly, right on top of radio station KRVN in Lexington came this strange voice in a conversational tone, not at all like the announcer: "This is K0UWK, Ainsworth." The voice continued talking to someone else about radio, the weather, and life in general. I was excited and worried. I thought someone was broadcasting illegally. I went to my favorite radio shop and inquired about it. I was given the name of the amateur radio operator. I called George, and my dad took me over to meet him. I was transfixed. Here was the most wonderful set of radio equipment I had ever seen: A large box with meters and many knobs, and a mike—the transmitter, and a smaller box with another meter and not quite so many knobs—the receiver.

I fell in love. I wanted to be able to do that—talk all over the country with other people. Here was a way to get out of my limited, painful situation, in a more active way than the listening I had done to faraway stations on the regular radio band.

I studied hard on the Morse Code requirement, learning from the records George loaned me. By the time school started, I had a good start. By late fall, I got up the courage to take the exam from a ham in Bassett, the next town east. By December, 1959, I had my first "ticket"—a "Novice" class license, KN0YDS. I bought a simple used transmitter (Heathkit DX-20), and an old receiver (Hallicrafters S-38) from a much younger ham in that town, and my dad put up a simple antenna.

I made my first call on January 15, 1960. I was answered right away. "KN0YDS DE KN0YBX" was the reply. It turned out to be Bob from Sturgis, South Dakota, another teenager, my same age. I was so excited and nervous on this first contact that on the second transmission that I sent a whole transmission, probably at least four minutes (sending at five words per minute!), without switching the antenna from the receiver to the transmitter. When I discovered my mistake and listened, Bob was calling me. I repeated it all again, this time with the antenna connected! We talked several times after that, and I even stopped by to visit him the next time we went to the Black Hills for our summer camping trip.

I made all my contacts by Morse code, since that's all the Novice license allowed. I eventually worked my speed up to 15 words per minute and took the tests for my next level, a "Conditional" class license, given by the same elderly ham in Bassett (W0WRY) who had administered my first tests. Eventually I got up to 20 words per minute and got a certificate recognizing that.

My first station was in the parsonage basement on a workbench table. This station's transmit switch was attached to a small piece of Masonite board just below the tabletop. I had set it up so that it would apply high voltage to the transmitter when

time to transmit, with a separate switch for the antenna. One day, in the middle of a conversation (by Morse code), when it came time to answer the other station, I reached down without looking to turn on the transmitter. Unfortunately, the switch was open on the back side of the board, and when I reached, my middle and fourth fingers touched the contacts on the switch. I received a nasty shock and got burned skin on the two fingertips of that hand! Thankfully, I was sitting on a wooden chair with my other hand resting on the wooden top of the desk, so the shock went only through those two fingers. I've had other shocks, but that one was certainly the most memorable! I became much more respectful of voltage after that. One rule hams use is to always have one hand in your pocket when working around voltage (even when the power is off).

Eventually, I moved the station up to my bedroom in the front of the Ainsworth parsonage using the same transmitter but a larger and more capable receiver that I got from an uncle in Arkansas. Dad and I engineered and he built a fifty-foot wooden pole attached to the back of the house for a wire antenna for the lowest band on which I could operate. I also built a voice adapter ("plate modulator") for the transmitter and used that for many enjoyable contacts mostly around Nebraska, and sometimes with some other high schoolers. One of them decided that my call sign stood for "Young Dashing Screwball." (I typically say these days that I'm less young, less dashing, and, hopefully, less screwy.)

In high school, I was active in message-handling, almost entirely by Morse code, and even served a couple of years as the main administrator and net control station for the main Nebraska National Traffic System network. I also was able to represent Nebraska on the regional traffic net (also by Morse code, though much faster!) My radio skills have greatly improved over the years to include some digital modes in addition to voice and code. I was active in the Amateur Radio Emergency Service off and on for years, first in Southern California during seminary and later in Colorado.

Ham radio for me provided some challenging learning opportunities for the technical side of radio and electronics. Putting a station together, especially in the early days, required knowledge of antennas, feedlines, switching, transmitters, receivers, and maintaining it all. It was a satisfying accomplishment. So, I did learn how to make radios run, and not only receivers, but transmitters as well!

College: "Free at Last"

College years were times of flowering, exploring—and being confused! I enrolled in Nebraska Wesleyan University (NWU), which offered a scholarship to ministers' kids. Dad drove me and my stuff from Ainsworth to the campus in Lincoln. As he drove away, I took a deep breath and breathed a big sigh of relief: "Free at last." My continuing development as a horn player and in my academic interests were where I flowered. I explored several fields as I generally enjoyed academic study. I was interested in physics first, then music education, then, briefly, church music, and finally pre-theology. Finding my future path was both my excitement and confusion.

During most of my college years, I had a work-study job with the library, verifying cataloging and ordering information. I think I got 50 cents an hour at first (1964!). I got to process most of the library of E. Glenn Callen, a recently-deceased long-time sociology professor there at Nebraska Wesleyan.

I did not go through the Greek system rush, choosing to remain independent, which continued to be my decision over the next couple of rush seasons. I questioned this at one point in my sophomore year, and I remember a friend in one of the Greek houses telling me it wasn't necessary since I'd made a good adjustment and to just keep on my path.

Even though I had enjoyed Methodist Youth Fellowship (MYF) and choir in Ainsworth, I felt I was done with church now that I was in college. I knew there was a chaplain and some kind of student religious group called the Methodist Student Movement (MSM), but I didn't want to participate. However, near the end of my first semester in the New Men's Dorm on campus, Norm, the president of the campus MSM, found me and told me that there was going to be a national gathering of the MSM in Lincoln over Christmas break, and he thought I might like it. It would have some big-name speakers and activities I might find interesting. So, I went.

I was inspired. Martin Luther King, Jr. spoke about non-violence. I heard sermons by James Matthews, and a speech by Bishop James Thomas, a black man assigned to all-white Iowa and one of the youngest to be elected bishop. I heard a memorable sermon entitled "The Cruciform Principle," which (as I think about it now) was, in a way, similar to a book theologian John Cobb wrote years later, *Christ in a Pluralistic Age*. It was historic for the MSM and for me. I was hooked. I became active in MSM and never looked back. My church career had begun.

In Nebraska when I was a student, MSM morphed into the University Christian Movement. I served on the Nebraska

United Ministries in Higher Education board as a college student, and on the first General Program Council of the new United Methodist Church in late college and early seminary as a young adult representative. One event I remember from this latter activity was a meeting where the logo of the new UMC was decided: a cross with two joined flames on the left side, symbolizing the joining of two spiritual communities: Evangelical United Brethren and Methodist, as well as Christ (cross) and the Holy Spirit (flames). FirstUMCLincoln.org (where we were married) has an image of the logo. (This logo is being questioned by some now, based on a greater awareness of the racism of the Methodist church that has led some to point out that flames on a cross are reminiscent of the burning crosses of the Jim Crow south!)

I was also active in student politics, running unsuccessfully for student body vice-president once and serving on the student senate. I had a reputation for being something of a student liberal, and was an active leader in MSM and University Christian Movement, both locally and statewide. I enjoyed the leadership experience.

A small group of students once developed a closed-circuit radio station. As I recall, I built a simple transmitter and engineered the closed-circuit campus wiring. It wasn't as "closed-circuit" as we thought: the FCC monitoring station in Grand Island heard us one day and demanded we cease operation! We were running only 50 watts into cables to the dorms! Oops! Not the best engineering, huh?

During my first year and into my second year of college, I dated a classmate who also played in the band. I really liked Mary and was quite attracted to her. She was a free spirit and helped me become more comfortable with erotic feelings and sensuality. The relationship was also significantly intimate emotionally. We spent some good times together, including on a band trip to Chicago to play the halftime show for a

Chicago Bears game. (A memorable moment of this halftime show was losing a slip-on shoe!) Another memorable experience on this trip was that she and I went to the top of the Prudential Building together, one of the tallest buildings in Chicago at the time, looking out over the city together. I enjoyed my time with her. My mother, however, was not so excited by this interest and encouraged me (pretty strongly) to look elsewhere, but I found it hard to distance myself from her, and I wasn't ready for the recriminations that would follow if I didn't do it.

During my sophomore year I roomed with Bill, a theatre major, who was always making design drawings of theatre set pieces. Right before Christmas break, he was producing a student-directed play, *The Dock Brief.* He asked me if I would escort his girlfriend to the play, since he was the director. I agreed; she was a nice young woman whom I had met because of him and whom I already liked. After the play, we were standing around waiting for him to finish closing up the Loft theatre. When he arrived, I was dismissed from my escort duties. There was another person, however, the script supervisor, hanging around after the production. Bill and his girlfriend Diane invited me and this other young woman named Margaret, or as she preferred, Maggie, to go to Harold's Place, just off campus for a malt. Well, I'll go almost anywhere for a malt, and I said sure.

Maggie and I hit it off during the walk over and back. I asked her out every night after that before I left for Christmas break— and she accepted! We dated all through the next semester. I broke up with her during the summer, taking an opportunity to test my feelings toward my first "flame" in asserting myself with mom. That lasted until my birthday: Mary and I were in the basement of the dorm when Maggie brought me a birthday card! That re-ignited my interest in her. The attempt to re-establish a relationship with Mary was enlightening, as I then saw more clearly the differences in the relationships, and decided to put my energies into the relationship with Maggie. We've been together ever since.

I always liked studying the English language. Harold Hall, the professor of the honors English class, was especially good and encouraged and helped me hone my writing skills. One assignment I wrote was about the experience of my friends running away from me in Bayard. I titled it "Little Benny" or something like that. He didn't like the word "Little." He still gave me a good grade, though.

Sometime early in my time at NWU, a new chaplain arrived named Jerry Walker. He was an energetic organizer and inspirational leader. He kept encouraging my questions and talking about a theologian he found very important and inspiring: theologian and ethicist Reinhold Niebuhr. He turned out to be an important person in my thinking and writing, even in seminary. These discussions and my involvement in MSM helped me when it came time to declare a major.

I was trying to decide what I wanted to do. Since I liked the sciences in high school and my ham radio experiences, perhaps I could be a scientist (actually more like an electronics engineer). I took physics and aced the class. Unfortunately, calculus never made any sense to me (why would you want to do science with approximations??), and it derailed my interest. So, since I was having a good time in music, I thought maybe I'd be a music major: I took horn lessons, and was enjoying playing first horn in the orchestra, but not until my last year or so was I able to land first horn in band. My last year, I played a horn solo at a band concert, and did very well with it. Nevertheless, when I honestly looked at what would be required to be a professional musician, I couldn't see myself in a practice room 8 hours a day. So, maybe I could teach.

By now, I was a junior. My first semester of an education class was disastrously boring. The deadline to declare a major was looming. I did some serious reflection: What really was interesting to me? What questions were most important to me? I decided that questions of "ultimate importance," those with which philosophy and religion dealt, were what were most important to me. So, I declared religion and philosophy as my major and music as my minor.

My first class in the religion department was exciting: contemporary theology, taught by Fred Blumer. It really captured my attention and interest. I wrote a paper on the "New Quest for the Historical Jesus." Dr. Blumer became an academic role model for his clarity of thought and openness to exploration and questioning. Unfortunately, the two classes on Old and New Testaments, taught by a much older professor, were no match. This professor seemed to represent much that I was questioning at that time, and even seemed to belittle some of my explorations. I struggled to stay interested in his classes. History of Christianity was a challenge because I was more interested in the history of the ideas, but the class required remembering the dates and the people. But I hung in and took a philosophy class, which was a challenge intellectually, especially trying to make sense of the "proofs" of the existence of God. I ended up graduating with a religion/philosophy major and a music minor. I wrote a major paper on the thought of Reinhold Niebuhr in one of my last classes. When it came time to write my major professional project in seminary, Niebuhr was the focus of the theological part of my writing.

Chaplain Jerry gave me encouragement and support for my social conscience expressions in Christian student movement activities, and in my academic pursuits. He also encouraged me to get a "different cultural experience" in attending seminary. I applied to Perkins, the University of Chicago Divinity School, and the School of Theology at Claremont. I eventually decided to go to Claremont. It turned out to be a good decision.

I combined my interest in music and engineering with Classical Hours programming and announcing, and logging transmitter parameters at KFMQ during my final years at Wesleyan. My voice and ease with reading aloud and my First Class Radiotelephone license for broadcast engineering got me a job as a newsreader and transmitter engineer with KECK southeast of Lincoln. A friend of mine, a fellow amateur radio operator and electronics engineering student at UN-L had recruited me to mind the station while he did a weekly remote broadcast at a furniture store. This station was a 5,000-watt country music station with a directional broadcast pattern (which required the First Class license). I had a brief stint at country DJ after school, but thankfully, that didn't last long! Country music wasn't my thing.

Decision to Enter Ministry

So, I grew up in a parsonage, surrounded by talk of church and faith, attending church every Sunday where dad led worship and preached. When we moved to Ainsworth, I sang in the choir, attended Methodist Youth Fellowship, and went to youth events. There wasn't one particular decision or influence but a series of smaller ones that led me to ministry.

I grew up listening to dad's sermons, sometimes from the back pew lying down and napping, nearly always with my mom and sister(s) on the same pew. Church, religion, and the people that went with them were almost daily parts of life. I saw more regularly and, at closer range than many, the humanness of the institution. Yet it was also the deep commitment of both of my parents to the best values of Christianity and social concern that inspired me. For all my problems in the relationship with my parents, their consistency and their perseverance with organizations that hurt and disappointed them spoke deeply to me. My dad always had a strong sense of justice, and sometimes got in trouble because of that: he spoke once in Ainsworth on Memorial Day, I think it was, or perhaps Veterans Day. He came home and said, "I think that's the last time I'll be asked to speak there." I don't remember why he thought that, but I know he was a pacifist, even though he didn't talk about it much. I think he probably didn't praise the country and its veterans strongly enough. I know he was a member of the Fellowship of Reconciliation, a liberal world peace organization. Mom wouldn't join, but I don't remember her rationale.

My mom's missionary impulse never died: we served for a few months as a foster family for three young Native American girls. She was always involved in the Women's Society of Christian Service (WSCS) when we were kids. After us kids were gone, she finished an education master's degree and began teaching special education. She was well-loved by her kids, though I cringed at the paternalistic way she talked about them.

There were two particularly important early experiences that shaped my Christian commitment. Membership classes and joining the church in sixth grade was one of those. It was a time when I felt close to God and felt quite serious about what kind of commitment this act meant.

The other was my experience with church camp, Methodist Youth Fellowship (MYF), and one particular district "midwinter institute" on dating. These were important to my religious development, helping my knowledge and experience of grace deepen. At one of the "midwinter institutes," held at the Methodist church in Wayne, Nebraska, I remember being puzzled and unsure about this commitment that people were asking of us as youth. I went into the sanctuary there, with its old, stately pipe organ and ornate architecture, and just sat. I had never heard God speak to me in words, like he seemed to speak to others, so it was pretty much a one-way conversation. It went something like this: "God, I don't know who you are, or what you are, but I do know that I want to commit myself to you and to your ways." That was a time of one of my major commitments, and one in which I continue to grow. I remember deciding at one camp experience that I was not going to fight with my sisters—and I pretty much stopped!

I was encouraged to preach in high school and did preach once on I Timothy 4:12 (on setting the believers an example as a youth). But I really didn't want to go into the ministry. This lasted into college, but in the middle of my junior year at Wesleyan, I changed to a religion-philosophy major, as I wrote about above. It had an immediate feeling of being right for me.

I am reminded of the line I read once about John Wesley, founder of Methodism. Peter Bohler, a young German Moravian Christian, said to him when he was questioning: "Preach faith until you have it." I feel like my development of faith has been something like that. I have known that at various times I have been preaching as much to myself as to others, and in counseling sometimes I have heard myself speak and realized I needed to apply my words in my own life. I feel oftentimes like a fellow traveler, sharing a journey with my parishioners or clients. I am more comfortable with this now, as I have been more able to affirm more completely my own humanness.

My reading, classwork, supervision, and moments of counseling and spiritual direction have all helped in my growth spiritually, as I see the larger picture, see my place in it, and see the work of healing happening around, in, and sometimes through me. I have continued to grow in my understanding of faith and its place in one's life. An appendix, written in 2019, speaks of these faith commitments after a painful 2019 General Conference. (A General Conference is a gathering of the worldwide United Methodist Church to decide issues and rules.)

Seminary

I graduated from NWU in May 1969 with Maggie and my sister Phyllis. In June, Maggie and I married, and we drove to Claremont, California, where I was to start seminary at the School of Theology at Claremont, now called Claremont School of Theology. Maggie started work at the seminary library. I started a job doing the night shift at an automated easy-listening FM station in Ontario, just down the road east of the school. My work was feeding large reels of recorded music to the automated music programming machine and reading news once an hour. During one of those newscasts, I even got to announce the 1969 moon walk! It was an eventful summer: the Stonewall Riots in New York City (though I was not paying much attention at the time) and the first landing on the moon. When classes started in September, I let that job go.

My knowledge and interest in electronics had gotten the attention of the faculty member responsible for the film, video, and sermon-taping area. I was asked to work as a maintenance technician in the media lab, learning videotape and film projection technology and maintaining the videotape recorder used for preaching classes. I agreed, and found the work challenging and enjoyable, with some occasional tension with the faculty supervisor.

Much of these years is somewhat of a blur as I look back. I think I might have been on a kind of overload. Some of the studying was just plain hard, hard to understand and hard to slog through. I almost dropped out near the end of the first semester of my second year, but a wise field placement and internship supervisor encouraged me to take a break with an internship at First Baptist, Los Angeles.

I did so, serving as a youth and young adult minister there. I was told it was an unusual American Baptist church in Southern California, an international, intercultural, and ecumenical congregation in the heart of the city. I found the work there challenging, enjoyable, and rewarding. I worked with kids and young adults of several races and ethnicities from the neighborhood. The kids came to an open gym on Saturday mornings. The young adults developed a slide show using the music of *Jesus Christ Superstar* and contemporary photos. I had the task of preparing young people in the sixth grade for baptism and church membership, which was an interesting experience for this Methodist who believed in infant baptism, and whose experience had not included baptism by immersion. It was a good experience all around. My supervising pastors were encouraging and affirming. They were helpful in giving me an inside look at caring, committed, and effective pastors of a large inner-city church. The experience bolstered my self-confidence and renewed my commitment to more study. It turned out to be just what was needed at that point in my life and education. I had a positive role in the church, and it had a positive impact on my confidence.

Claremont was not known as a hotbed of social activism in the seventies. One project a group of us did late one night was this banner, hung on the nearly-completed chapel building. I painted at least one letter. Tires screeched on Foothill Boulevard the next morning. We learned that the scaffolding that enabled the climbers among us to hang it was due to be removed the next day.

A highlight of my years at Claremont included coursework with John Cobb and my excitement at the discovery of process theology. Process theology is a way of looking at life, reality, and theology that sees all as an interconnected web of occasions and events. My classes with him were a huge influence: I found his perspective of process theology and that of Charles Hartshorne to be most enlightening. They made a lot of sense to me, though the specialized language and terms were sometimes confusing and puzzling.

Because of my experience of complete loss of control over my body and my life from polio and its treatment, process theology feels like liberation. Self-determination and free will are key features of process theology: Everything in the universe is in a process of change and becoming. God is not eternally unchanging, immovable, all-powerful, and coercive, but instead has a persuasive power to influence, rather than control. God is also influenced by what happens in the world, in a similar way that a lover is influenced by the beloved. What I do matters and has an impact on God. The focus is on becoming rather than being: Everything in the universe is in a process of "becoming" rather than just "being." The universe is in God and God is in everything, but everything is not God. Thus the term panentheism is an accurate description of this type of theology. (Wikipedia's article would be a good starting place to learn about this complex way of looking at reality and human existence.) Dr. Cobb had a depth of faith, humanness, and lack of pretense about him that spoke deeply to me.

Seminary faculty were particularly influential for me, including Frank Kimper in pastoral counseling, an amazing man: sensitive, deep, caring, and who introduced me to gestalt therapy. Ethicist Dan Rhoades had the courage of his principles, an openness to vigorous academic and social debate, and was a positive role model for me. I enjoyed his class on theological ethics. He had a major influence on my choice to embrace contextual ethics, evidence of which you can see in my writings on sexuality. He was also my faculty advisor and helped greatly in the final weeks before graduation.

Other faculty members were both an inspiration and a challenge to me. Jack Coogan, in the arts, worship, and liturgy, shaped my philosophy, planning and leadership of congregational worship. Rolf Knierim taught me the discipline of careful biblical interpretation, especially form criticism. I learned about stages of personal and faith development from Paul Irwin, which eventually helped me see the value of developmental psychology, and led me much later to the thought of Ken Wilber.

Weekly chapel was a very rich experience for me. Instead of the high drama and hymns of the seasonal celebrations that meant a lot to me, this was a time of quiet devotion. Though it was a liturgically high service, it was intimate, with spoken prayers, bidding prayers, and informal homilies. It was always the same service, somewhat in the Episcopal tradition. The hymns were chosen at the time of the service by the pianist and liturgist. The pianist was a student there, too, and could play them with zest, and volume. He insisted that most hymns should be sung at the speed of the poetry that they accompanied. They were often the same hymns, and I came to love them—I still get goose bumps from "Deck Thyself, My Soul, With Gladness." There was a very warm spirit among the little community who regularly gathered.

In my quest to work out the puzzle of human sexuality, I wrote several papers on various aspects of human sexuality and marriage. There was a class in film taught by Jim Wall for which I wrote a paper on whether the movie *Unfolding* by Constance Beeson was obscene (I decided that it was sensitively and explicitly erotic, but it wasn't obscene, but couldn't be used in a church). I got a positive response from Dr. Wall. For a class on social issues, I and two other students wrote a paper about marriage, sexuality, and "extramarital affairs." My part in it was to write a theological ethical perspective. I don't recall that it generated a lot of positive affirmation! (My recent reading of it and a related similar paper shows how deeply indebted my thought at that time was to German theologian Helmut Thielicke, who focused his *Ethics of Sex* (1964) on the biblical concept of the binary sexual differentiation of male and female, a concept I now find doesn't match what science is discovering about the complexity of biology, genetics, and endocrinology of sex differentiation. I also wrote a paper on "The History of the Marriage Ceremony to 1563" for worship class. For church history, I wrote on John Calvin's ideas on human sexuality and a brief commentary on Luther's *Marriage Booklet for Simple Pastors*. Looking over these writings and the professors' comments, I wasn't a star student, but I did learn a lot.

The Doctor of Ministry degree required an extensive "professional project" (they had stopped calling it a "dissertation" by then). I wanted to write about sexuality, and my advisors finally accepted the idea that I could compare and contrast sex education curricula for youth in the Southern California United Methodist Church and the Unitarian Universalist Church from a theological perspective based on the thought of Reinhold Niebuhr, the theologian I had gotten to know from Wesleyan days. Niebuhr's thought was helpful in giving a structure to my ethical framework, but his theology was more traditional than I really believed. But reading the theological section of that now, I find it one of my best writing efforts of that era.

A class on sexuality ministry had the choice of writing a paper or attending the National Sex Forum in San Francisco. I chose the latter and Maggie and I (and our dog Sandy) drove to San Francisco for the weeklong class. The experience was eye-opening to the varieties of human sexual behavior and how people felt about what they were doing. Panel discussions and multimedia presentations were the main methods. I was introduced to the spectrum of sexual orientation, which would come in handy later.

I helped with the youth ministry at Claremont UMC, and for a class assignment, I decided to interview several of them for a video on their thoughts on sexuality. It involved manually editing the session video on the one-inch open-reel videotape machines we were using. It was a meaningful time for them and for me. I still like the closing theme song I used, by the group Bread, "Make It with You."

Maggie enrolled in the Master of Library and Information Science program at UCLA in 1973. While she was at library school and we lived in LA during my last two years in seminary, I was a videotape, film, and control room engineer with Theta Cable Television in Santa Monica. I would work in the UCLA library on my final "professional project" and then drive out to Santa Monica to serve as the engineer for the 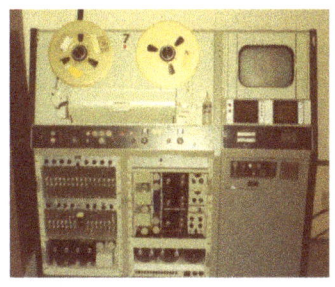 video productions of the public access channel and playback engineer for the premium movie channel. I enjoyed working with both half-inch- and one-inch-wide format open-reel videotape and the large two-inch-wide format Ampex "quad" tape machines. I had to (or got to) watch many movies. Most memorable: *Death Wish* and *Dirty Harry* (neither pleasant to watch); and *Blazing Saddles,* a real hoot to watch all eight times it ran! The chief engineer was a friendly guy and worked collaboratively with the engineers on staff. I enjoyed this job. One fun experience was when one of us complained that we couldn't get the big Ampex quad videotape machine to work. After poking around on the electronics, someone suggested checking whether it was plugged in. Rolling the machine out away from the wall, we discovered it had been unplugged! End of problem.

I enjoyed my technical work at Theta Cable. Besides being a source of income, it was a source of satisfaction, proving to myself that I could use my interest in technology and get paid for it! I had learned how radio worked. Now, I understood how television worked, and could even evaluate the technical quality of the movies we were showing.

Maggie had one of her most satisfying jobs at the UCLA library government documents department. After she would get off work at nine p.m., I'd drive back to UCLA, pick her up, and we'd often go to the (by then nearly deserted) Will Rogers Beach near Santa Monica and watch the waves, relax, talk, and catch up.

It was a time of growing spirituality for me, though at the time, I was barely able to articulate just what it meant to me. I had some of the language to talk intellectually about it, but I now recognize the deeper level that was touched within me.

I had a couple of friends in seminary who were particularly significant to me: one was my immediate supervisor in the media lab. Another friend was another fellow student with whom I would spend time. We would talk for long periods of time, bouncing ideas off each other, trying out connections between various parts of our learnings. His companionship was fun and satisfying.

I almost didn't graduate in 1975. I had done a paper for one of the professors, and turned it in a couple of hours late, as I recall. He wouldn't accept it because it was late. I was devastated, and at a final student group gathering at Dan Rhoades' home, I broke down and told him what had happened. I was forced to trust him. My father was on his way to our graduations, mine and Maggie's a week later, and to help us pack for our move back to my first church in southeast Nebraska. Dr. Rhoades took up my case with the other professor, and was able to resolve the issue, to my huge relief and deep gratitude for him.

THREE

Ministry ... and Burnout

We returned to Nebraska after seminary for my first ministerial appointment (assignment). It was in southeast Nebraska, as associate pastor to a five-church "larger parish" centered around First UMC in Fairbury, with another pastor as senior minister. I had primary administrative and ministry responsibilities for two of the smaller churches, including the one in the town in which we lived, Endicott, a small town of about 160 people about five miles southeast of Fairbury. I preached every Sunday at Endicott and Diller churches, once a month at Fairbury and the open-country church Helvey, and every other Sunday at Reynolds. I also had responsibility for education, youth, and social concerns at the largest church in Fairbury. I led confirmation classes for youth at the Fairbury and Endicott churches to learn about the United Methodist Church and decide whether they would confirm their membership for themselves. One of my successes was working with world hunger with a small group of members of the parish churches. One of the educational experiences was a simulation meal showing the various levels of food use: from barely scraping by with minimal food to middle-class folks eating out and paying for service to wealthy people with servants.

Endicott was a large producer of bricks from the clay hills south of town. We lived in the Endicott parsonage, a delightful brick house a block from the church, also of brick. The Endicott church had been served for four years by a conservative, non-Methodist minister (with the approval of the Nebraska UM conference, of course). I was told that they weren't so sure they wanted to be United Methodist. I took that as a challenge and worked hard to show the benefits of being UM. My first year there, my senior pastor and I had some tensions: he told me that he saw his job as "taking that seminary stuff out of you"! I was also greeted with some suspicion: "Why, you're just a kid" (said one church member). Having California plates on my "foreign" (Datsun) car didn't help either (and it didn't seem to make any difference that the automatic transmission was made by Borg Warner in Michigan). A second senior pastor, Nye Bond, and I worked well together, and we helped keep the parish a viable entity at one critical point. He was one of the two best supervisors I ever had. I had a deep respect for him: he was one of the freedom riders in Selma. He was centered, clear eyed, a truly grounded liberal Christian minister who knew how to manage conflict and a green associate minister! In him I saw caring, committed, and effective ministry again, and was coached effectively. My talents were honored, challenged, and encouraged. I grew a lot and I felt like I was helpful to this church.

I developed a practice of preaching from small 3x5 cards, which usually had most of a manuscript text. In my sermons, I enjoyed trying to make connections between the lectionary Biblical texts assigned for a given Sunday and contemporary issues. Of course, I had helps: besides the usual commentaries, knowledge and skill to fix things like this. The continuation of my childhood and adolescent interest in technology had saved me bunches of trouble and money.

I remember this was also during the debate over the Briggs Initiative in California—I put a sign in the window encouraging a vote against it! This initiative was a California ballot proposition proposed by state legislator John Briggs that would have banned gay and lesbian people from working in California schools. This was a significant turning point in the Bay Area's queer history. Opposition to the proposition was swift, passionate, and creative. Queer people canvassed, wrote letters to the editors, and came out to loved ones and neighbors in order to teach the public that they were already a part of civic and professional life. Harvey Milk was instrumental in defeating Briggs, and by the end of the campaign, even ex-governor Ronald Reagan voiced public opposition to the measure, which was defeated by a margin of 58.4% to 41.6%. (GLBTHistory.org, retrieved 5/26/2023)

I was excited to be there at this time and watch this success. I was so hopeful it was the start of greater acceptance of LGBTQ people. But that process would take years...

The experience at the Institute was a wonderful time of learning about the breadth of human sexuality and how the humans who participated in it felt about what they were doing. Near the end of the time, Maggie joined me in the "Sexual Attitude Restructuring" experience, an intensive exploration of sexuality in lecture and workshops with a large group. This experience was a further confirmation of my sexual orientation of what I was calling at the time bisexuality. I came home with an Instructor in Human Sexuality certificate.

As part of my process to clarify my desire in 1979 to do ministry in the area of human sexuality, I attended a summer class in 1980 at Iliff School of Theology with James B. Nelson, author of the book, *Embodiment: An Approach to* and music tapes to keep me company. I felt a sense of elation as I drove, a sense of excitement at this new "adventure." I was in a reflective mood the whole time. I drove listening to music that I had liked a lot in seminary, which included the monks of Weston Priory, *Jonathan Livingston Seagull*, and *Music for Organ, Brass and Percussion*.

One place I stopped was at a scenic overlook on Interstate 80 near the Sherman Mountains in Wyoming. It was a thrill to see the Rockies. I had the sense of a dream coming true. I wrote, "This trip is only the major part: representing a growing appreciation for myself and who I am and what I have to offer."

This trip was a milestone in my journey to be more "me." It was eventful: I drove until I got tired and slept until I awoke, rested, and took my time. The scenery was inspiring, and it was a wonderful feeling of being free, an unusual feeling in my history up to then. I spent a little time in Salt Lake City but wasn't in a sight-seeing mood. As I drove into Nevada, the "charge" light came on. I got out the factory service manual for the car to see what was wrong. The alternator had gone out. I read the manual and realized I had the tools and the knowledge to fix it. I figured out that I could probably drive far on just the battery, and probably could get to Reno, where I could get the required part (diodes). So, I had a service station charge the battery and drove on. I monitored the battery voltage as I drove, to be sure I had enough current. I picked up the part in Reno, and continued driving. I got through Sacramento, but I had to turn on the lights, as it was getting dark. The battery voltage went down rapidly. I got to the Bay area, as far as the north bridge when it died. I was towed by a state tow truck (I was on state property) to a nearby service station. I spent the night in the car, coasted down a hill one block to the gas station, and had the alternator removed, repaired, and remounted before the station opened up. I got started and was on my way again, with dirty hands and tears in my eyes giving thanks for the

Maggie had begun work as a regional library coordinator with the Nebraska Library Commission, and in 1979, because of my part-time work (and salary), I started working at the Commission myself as a media technician with audio recording and maintenance responsibilities. I monitored and recorded the reading of books and other materials for what used to be called the library for the blind and physically handicapped. This involved running the open-reel tape recorder and making real-time edits when a reader made a mistake. I also helped maintain the bulk cassette tape duplicator and keep records. It provided some low-stress income and a job I found meaningful.

Career Assessment and Recovery

My part-time job at this parish gave me some space while I figured out what I really wanted to do, since parish ministry was so stressful. As a result of my leaving my first appointment and in deep questioning about my future directions, I decided to do a career assessment process in Minnesota and to read and do all the exercises in the book *What Color Is Your Parachute?* (Bolles, 1978) The outcome of this process was to awaken a desire to do more professionally with my interest in sexuality.

Part of my career assessment and this desire to do more in the area of sexuality was a trip to San Francisco in the summer of 1978. This was a significant experience in my life. I had just begun a year's leave of absence from full-time ministry. The trip was to be a six-week period of training in human sexuality education at the Institute for Advanced Study of Human Sexuality. The trip had been planned since late February when I attended a workshop there as a way of seeing if sexuality work was for me. It had been planned out of my need to reflect on my future as a minister and what the shape of my ministry was to be. I planned to stay at a friend's apartment in Berkeley.

The drive from Lincoln to San Francisco itself was very meaningful. I was driving alone, with a ham radio transceiver

FOUR

The Lincoln Era

We moved to Lincoln in 1978, with me nearly burned out, after ending my first appointment as associate minister in rural southeast Nebraska. I then worked part-time as an education minister with the "PEACe" Parish, a cooperative parish of Palmyra, Eagle, Aldersgate and Cheney United Methodist Churches east of Lincoln. I did youth work and teacher training for church school teachers, as I recall. It was a rewarding association with another creative woman clergy colleague, Susan Davies. Maggie and I were active in Aldersgate, a small progressive congregation in southeast Lincoln, with a round sanctuary that was frequently decorated with new designs based on the church year from a team that consisted of artistic folks like the pastor's spouse David Davies. The designs were amazing, often profound, and enriched the worship experiences led by Susan. I remember a Good Friday service where it felt like we were entering a dark tomb—and then on Easter it was a huge contrast of brilliant light and color!

course, involves much more than just the mechanics, and more creativity than most animals can muster!

After nearly three years as a parish pastor, it was clear I had difficulty making priority decisions in the administration work, however, and approached burnout. But it was also in the summer and fall of 1977 when I became more clearly aware of my attraction to a male friend. This became a crisis, which is discussed in the section below, "Sexuality: The Puzzle." I took a leave of absence relationship from the denomination from June, 1978, to January, 1981 and we moved to Lincoln.

I had a collection of small booklets keyed to the common lectionary texts, which often had helpful suggestions from which I spun off my thoughts. One of my Easter sermons used a visual aid. I went to the Endicott trash dump and got an old beat-up milk can and had a church member who was good with flowers put an arrangement on the lid. I think the title was "Speechless at Easter."

One of the most difficult sermons I wrote came two days after my sister Becky died suddenly from systemic lupus erythematosus and a burst aortic aneurysm on Good Friday, 1978, just weeks before we moved to Lincoln. Believe me, it was a challenge to preach that Easter morning sermon! But I did it, and I think it was not a bad effort.

During these years, I was also involved in district youth and Christian education work. As part of this, I helped provide experiences in Christian education training for teachers in church school. I found I enjoyed worship leadership and preaching, and was helpful in facilitating organizational change for a broader participation of members. On the conference level, I used my experience with small-format videotape to edit a video program on the Family Farm, written and narrated by a woman clergy colleague at a church about 30 miles away. Also at the conference level, I was part of the genesis of a committee somewhat euphemistically called "Human Identity and Relationships," which developed sexuality education for all ages.

When one of the church members heard I was working with sexuality education with the conference, he remarked that he could be helpful: all I had to do was bring them out to his farm and he'd show them all they needed to know about sexuality! (I now don't think he was being serious, but I was so surprised I didn't know how to respond.) Human sexuality, of

Sexuality and Christian Theology (1978). That book had been incredibly important to my development of the theology of ministry in the area of human sexuality. The class was another experience confirming my career direction, especially with the affirmation of Jim Nelson and conversations around the edges of the class. One in particular was with a friend, Paula Murphy, a psychotherapist involved with sexuality issues in the Rocky Mountain Conference, who listened patiently to my wonderings about a ministry in human sexuality. Finally, she said, "Why don't you just do it?"

So, I began researching what it would take, from the point of view of the church: a rationale, an accountability structure, a vote by the Board of Ordained Ministry, and appointment by the bishop. I ended up writing an eight-page rationale for "A Ministry in Human Sexuality." (I wanted it to be taken seriously. I had been advised by some colleagues in ministry with whom I'd talked about the possibility, "Don't call it that.") A friend on the Board told me it was the longest and most complete rationale that had been presented for a "ministry beyond the local church," which was the phrase for these kinds of ministries in those days. In January 1981, the bishop affirmed my proposal and appointed me to a Ministry in Human Sexuality as a ministry "beyond the local church," as I had proposed. No salary was provided with the assignment other than what I could arrange from fundraising and client fees. Much more about this ministry is in its own section in Part II below.

As Ministry in Human Sexuality (MHS) developed, I left the Library Commission and took a part-time interim ministry at Ebenezer United Church of Christ, which included preaching, pastoral care, and preparing youth for confirmation in the UCC. In October 1982, the church found its permanent minister, and MHS became my full-time work.

I enjoyed teaching two college classes: human sexuality in the human services department at Southeast Community

College in Lincoln, and a class for the College of St. Mary of Omaha's Lincoln campus.

In Lincoln, we were active in various activities of the gay and lesbian communities. We helped start a chapter of Parents Families and Friends of Lesbians and Gays ("PFLAG Cornhusker").

The sponsorship of an appearance in 1981 by the San Francisco Gay Men's Chorus at First-Plymouth Congregational Church UCC, a block from where we lived at the time gave a huge burst of activism in Lincoln. For me, it was a huge inspiration and deeply moving experience. Out of those times was born a Gay and Lesbian Information and Support telephone help line, for which we both volunteered. Maggie was at one point the coordinator.

Community of Grace (COG)

One of the achievements I feel especially good about when we were in Lincoln was our leadership in developing a house church called "Community of Grace: An Interdenominational Worshipping [sic] Community of Lesbians and Gays and Others Identified With Us." In my work with feminist thought and theology, I had developed a commitment to non-hierarchical leadership styles, including decision-making by consensus. I had found an article on a modified consensus model developed by the National Lesbian Feminist Organization (1980). The rationale pointed out the need for new ways of making decisions that were not hierarchical. We adapted this and used it throughout the life of the church.

I had also become a strong advocate for inclusive language liturgy and hymns, and advocated strongly for the use of the songbook *Everflowing Streams* which was used as the "hymnal;" other times, we used song sheets of individual inclusive-language songs and hymns.

Community of Grace (COG) was a small group of people, many of whom were involved in their own "mainline" congregation on Sunday mornings but who came together to worship on Sunday evening to be safe with a community of people who identified with lesbians and gays. I encouraged us to model the community as a kind of "Para-Base Church," defined as a "small group of persons who, because of a specific concern, are drawn out of two or more congregations and across denominational lines." This kind of group "provides a supportive climate for persons who have special concerns with which the local establishment may or may not be in sympathy." (Olsen, 1973)

The community ranged in size from five to 40 over its lifespan, with occasional special events drawing over 40people. There was a coordinating committee for most of the years; general community meetings and a steering committee gave direction at other times.

Community of Grace had a kind of loosely non-clerical (as opposed to anti-clerical) leadership style, in part because there were several clergy who were regular participants and leaders, and in part because of the belief that leadership was to be shared, based on a particular person's gifts, not their standing as clergy or lay. But I'll always treasure the Pentecost service we held at a member's home alongside the swimming pool with seven clergy decked out with special bright yellow rainbow stoles made by a lesbian nurse, spanning a spectrum of faith traditions from United Methodist, Evangelical, and Ukrainian Orthodox celebrating communion. I treasure the stole I wore as clergy then (which Maggie occasionally wears now).

The worship style was highly variable and diverse by design: the traditions and personal preferences of participants varied from high Anglican and Orthodox to Methodist to Evangelical to contemplative traditions. A rotation of leaders, a mix of committed lay and clergy, was worked out so that the styles would balance out over a period of several weeks. By the leadership, one could know generally what style the service would be. It was a rich mix.

One of the more evangelical leaders encouraged us to write a covenant early on in the life of the group. As I recall, I then adapted it for use in worship settings. The diverse theological and denominational backgrounds of the participants made developing this a very interesting and delicate process. He wrote a first draft, and then a couple of small groups worked on sections and made a recommendation to the whole group. It was accepted with surprisingly little disagreement.

As a regularly worshiping and supportive community, I think COG provided some stabilizing influence during Lincoln's controversial consideration of an equal rights initiative in the early 80s, as well as some leadership in the formation of the Coalition for Lesbian and Gay Civil Rights.

Who attended? There were clergy who identified as gay, lesbian, and bi but who could not afford to be "out." There were laity who identified with lesbian and gay people but who themselves were either parents or were non-gay in orientation. There were lesbian, gay, and bi people who did not feel comfortable in any of the congregational options in the city at the time. And there were those who worshiped regularly in their "regular" congregations. COG was an important part of our life in Lincoln.

I wrote about this group as an example of "Church at the Margins," from Dan Spencer's article in *Christianity and Crisis,* vol. 52, no. 8 (May 25, 1992). I submitted this paper for an Iliff School of Theology class called "Historical And Contemporary Perspectives On Justice And Peace Struggles: Lesbian, Gay, And Bisexual Issues." It is on my personal website.

We had many gay and lesbian friends in Lincoln, and would occasionally drive to Omaha to dance at The Max, a great gay-friendly dance venue. One night, we drove with a gay man dressed as a woman and experienced his feelings of vulnerability in a time of legal and societal prejudice against cross-dressing.

In 1987, my dad died. My griefwork led to my decision to leave MHS and my encouraging Maggie to find more satisfying work than the series of short-term and less-than-fulfilling jobs she had had. She was in Washington, D.C. in 1988 for an Affirmation board meeting and mentioned she was looking for better work. A person who worked for Bread for the World (BFW), a hunger advocacy organization based in D.C., suggested she apply for an open position there. She did, and got the job!

FIVE

Denver: Go West!

So, we were going to move to Washington, D.C., where Maggie had gotten a regional organizing job with Bread For The World (BFW). Before I was able to get our household ready for the move, an opening in Denver became available and we decided to move west! We were both excited about this development. The move began a process of recovery and survival after MHS closed in February 1988, after 7 years.

We found an 1896 Victorian house for rent in the Baker Neighborhood, a near-downtown neighborhood with a mix of houses, apartments, duplexes, and 1890s "Painted Ladies" Victorian houses. It was also a mix of a diverse population racially, ethnically, and sexualities. We moved there with a couple who we'd been friends with in Lincoln and shared the household for several months while

they found a place for themselves. We eventually bought it and lived there 32 years.

We would often go up into the mountains west of Denver, usually up "Sq**w Pass Road" to Echo Lake and then down to Idaho Springs, where we might have dinner or a root beer float at the drive-in. The scenery was spectacular, looking north of the road clear to Longs Peak across the valleys and intervening hills. In the fall, the turning aspen trees were wonderful. We sometimes would stop at one of the picnic areas after "Sq**w Pass" and walk to an overlook. The mountain called "Sq**w Mountain" has now been renamed Mestaa'ėhehe (pronounced MES-ta-hay) Mountain as part of a "process of acknowledging the harm and trauma of the past and bridging the way for a peaceful future together." The mountain, located in Arapaho and Roosevelt National Forests, is named after a prominent Native woman in Colorado history: Mestaa'ėhehe in the Cheyenne language, also known as Owl Woman. (RMPBS)

Warren Church

We found a church in the Capitol Hill neighborhood, Warren UMC, with an old English-style sanctuary, a progressive pastor, and a heart for service. This church was instrumental in the 1970s in establishing Warren Village, a residential community next to the church for single parents. It, like most inner-city churches, was in decline and was looking for ways to serve the neighborhood with declining membership and a building dating from 1909. We had a hard time attracting and keeping folks with a similar interest in service and progressive faith. We tried to be a very warm, friendly community of faith with an outreach to unhoused people, LGBT folks, and the community at large. We were a friendly progressive church that took the Bible seriously but not literally.

In fact, in 1999 we became a Reconciling Congregation in the Reconciling Ministries Network. It was somewhat controversial at the start, but it was interesting that the vote came within weeks of a denominational Judicial Council ruling that churches could not call themselves "Reconciling." This gave a boost to the independent-minded members who took offense at the ruling and voted in favor of the move to public identification. The church had long been welcoming and inclusive of LGBTQ persons and, in fact, had been the meeting site for the Men's Coming Out Being Out support group for many years. Pastors were known to perform covenant services for couples of the same sex—which were, of course, not reported in the yearly reports.

One project that came near the end of the church's life was a shelter for homeless women. This caused some consternation among some neighbors. It strained the church's resources and spirit, since we weren't well prepared to handle the issues that came with some of the women we tried to serve.

Since we were open to groups who were welcoming to LGBTQ persons, we were approached by a couple of more evangelical but welcoming congregations who wanted to use the building for services: a Korean church and a Mongolian Church. A highlight of the Christmas Eve service in 2002, was that these two congregations and Warren people joined together for worship in four languages (Korean, Mongolian, English, and AMESLAN, American Sign Language)! Soon after that, another church with a primarily gay and lesbian congregation, Open Door, began meeting in the building. Scheduling was interesting! The income from these groups wasn't much, but we felt we were following our mission. The Korean church found another place closer to their community, so they didn't stay long. But Open Door stayed a number of years before moving to First Baptist Church nearby.

Warren folks participated in the Glide Empowerment Journey at Glide UMC in San Francisco, hoping to gain some ideas for ministry in our urban setting. A food pantry and a "Healing Story Circle" were started, but my sense was that the initial meetings of the Circle were too emotionally heavy for folks, so it was short-lived. The experience deepened our desire to do neighborhood ministry, but we didn't seem to have the resources to do it.

Various studies were offered, including *Living the Questions* and a Bible study, *Companions in Christ: The Way of Grace*. Three pastors were especially helpful, in our experience: Paul Kottke, who welcomed us the first Sunday we attended and heard and honored our pleas, "We're exhausted after our move to Denver and need some space to regroup." Paul was deeply involved in community ministry, and we were not ready to say good-bye when the bishop appointed him to University Park UMC in Denver. Eun-sang Lee brought a deepening spiritual emphasis to the congregation, and Mariah Hayden brought an energetic burst of hope, but, in the end, we couldn't financially support her full-time work, and when she left, we began to acknowledge the handwriting on the wall. We were spending down the endowment, which was not a good idea according to the conference, so that stopped and we were given a retired minister, Darrell Mount, who was tasked with helping us close in a meaningful way. He did that very well, bringing a world of experience, empathy, understanding, and knowledge.

We continued to worship at Warren until, in 2014, after we'd been there for 26 years, it finally closed after decades of decline. I held a number of positions in the congregation, including chair of a mission-vision team, chair of the administrative council, and chair of the board of

trustees. This last was tasked with the arrangements of closing the church and readying it for transfer to the United Methodist Rocky Mountain Conference. It was traumatic for us all as the church had a history of over 100 years! As we left, we wrote a proposal for the church to be developed as a service center for Capitol Hill and we were pleased when, ultimately, it was sold to the St. Francis Center and turned into a residential building for many homeless people.

Survival

I had begun the process of becoming a member of the AAPC late in my time in Lincoln and had worked with an AAPC supervisor, as required. When we first arrived in Denver in 1988, I tried to develop a counseling practice, first with Hope Care and Counseling, and then with St. Patrick's Counseling. I was never able to develop enough of a practice to make a living. During this work, I worked with a couple of other AAPC supervisors and eventually gained pastoral counselor-in-training membership. This ended in 1994, when the AAPC thought I didn't understand the gravity of a counseling boundary violation I had made. Related to this incident, in 1996, I surrendered my ministerial credentials to the Nebraska Conference.

While I tried to get the counseling practice started in Denver in 1988, I went to Kelly Services for a job that would provide some income. Because I typed 69 words per minute and knew WordStar, I got a job with a company that manufactured air pollution monitoring equipment and systems (Continuous Emission Monitoring Systems, or CEMS), typing price quotations for prospective customers. After several months, they bought out the Kelly Services contract and hired me. A new phase in my life began.

When they discovered I knew something about spreadsheets, something I had learned at MHS, they started having me work with their sales spreadsheets. My reputation spread, and one day the vice president of engineering recruited me to be his executive secretary. He said that his previous secretary kept messing up his engineering spreadsheet every month and he had to spend hours fixing it. I worked for two engineering VPs in that job. One of my tasks was putting together engineering manuals for the data acquisition systems. They were usually a minimum of a two-inch heavy binder, and sometimes three and four inches! Heavy.

One day while I was in this job, I heard about an opening for an "applications programmer" for the company's Xenix-based data acquisition computer system (DAS). This type of computer application collects data from smokestack gas analyzers that monitor various combustion products and stores it for later reporting. As it was around the time of the AAPC process, I decided it would help me through the stress of dealing with the AAPC because it would be a challenge to learn and would take a lot of concentration. So, I applied, and got the job! It was indeed a challenge, but I proved I could do it, and it helped me deal with the loss of my (formal) ministry.

The main problem with that job when I first took it was that the programmers were on the second floor of the second building on the two-building complex. By this time, I was using my first scooter, which meant I needed to walk up the stairs at least once a day and figure out how to do bio breaks! The two buildings were not on the same level of the property, and this second building was lower than the main one. One day when I was going from the main building to the second one down the hill, I decided to see what would happen if I coasted down the hill in my scooter! So, I took the brake off and started off. It started going very fast by the time we reached the bottom of the hill, and I was so thankful there was a level area at the bottom where the delivery trucks turned around! It coasted to a gentle stop. I never did that again. (The company eventually moved the department into the main (accessible) building.)

I worked with customers wherever in the world they might be, usually by phone and modem, to configure, modify, or fix problems with their DAS. In the United States, this was usually power plants and other sites that had some combustion process that the Environmental Protection Agency (EPA) and state air quality regulatory agencies require monitoring. So I had to learn EPA Parts 60 and 75 regulations.

One big project I did was a watershed for me. I had been assigned to configure the DAS for four power plants in Illinois. They were all very similar in the way the measuring instruments were laid out, and in the EPA regulations that governed them, which meant the software configurations would be similar. Well, it turns out I made similar errors in all four systems, and when I found out, it was discouraging, needless to say. Management decided to send me out to the field to fix all the errors to the satisfaction of the customer. As I started working on troubleshooting and fixing things, I felt a significant shift in my internal process: instead of getting bogged down in self-blame and self-denigration, I found myself saying (even out loud), "Well, let's see what's going on and what I need to do to fix it." The trip was a big success, with happy customers at all four sites. I enjoyed working with the folks who were charged with the EPA reporting. Dealing with EPA regulations and reporting wasn't always a fun job, of course. One of them told me she felt like the initials, CEM (Continuous Emission Monitoring), stood for "Career-Ending Move."

I had begun using a scooter to get around and was using an accessible van to travel to the four sites. At the oldest one on the banks of a big river, the generator floor and the floor with the DAS computer were on the second floor of this big old building. There was no internal elevator, but they did have an open external one. That was a real trip to ride!

Another adventure during my time at that company was a similar type of trip to the Virgin Islands, where two of the islands had our monitoring equipment at their power plants. The welcome was warm (as was the weather!), and I was always asked whether things were accessible enough. And I could honestly say yes. I had rented a van, asking that the middle seat be removed so I could get my scooter inside. I had taken a five-foot aluminum folding ramp on the plane, which worked pretty well to get me in. This was in the early days of 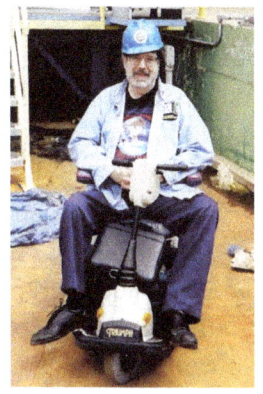 my scooter use, when I was much more able to walk and lift. They had handicapped parking places with signs that prohibited non-handicapped use with a fine of $1,000! I was able to get to the necessary equipment rooms without incident and was able to work well with the two young men who were in charge of the emissions monitoring, and provide more training for them.

I eventually got good enough that I became the main trainer and customer support for customers on this data acquisition system computer. I enjoyed teaching the classes with the CEMS personnel, who had varying levels of skill and knowledge. This gave me a challenge to explain something at various levels of detail. I became pretty good at Unix system administration for the DAS and enjoyed it a lot. I learned much about pollution monitoring and steam-powered electricity generation.

I was trained as an ISO 9001 internal auditor and helped develop and maintain a process for continuous quality improvement in the software services department based on the ISO 9001 standard, which is a certification in quality compliance and improvement. This was one time when my perfectionism was useful, if annoying for those who didn't want to work to established procedures! Luckily, I've grown since then and have reduced my perfectionism to near-negligible levels, though I still like to do whatever I'm doing well...

When the company changed to a Windows-based DAS using the SQL language, I struggled with this program and the Windows system itself and eventually left the company in 2000. Even so, I feel good about the work I did for this company. Over-all, it was a good phase of my life. Besides making good money, I enjoyed working with the technology: It gave me a sense of my power to master something difficult and technical. I grew significantly in my self-confidence and, of course, knowledge of technology. And I got to see the challenges of working in a corporate environment.

Back in the Church

We had a series of deaths in our families, starting with Maggie's mom Merna in 2000, my sister Phyllis in 2001, my mom in 2002, and my mom's sister Carol in 2003.

Maggie's mom had been declining since her husband Larry, Maggie's dad, had died.

Given my distant relationship with my own family, I had found it hard to get close to her parents, though I respected them both very much.

My aunt Carol, my mom's older sister didn't have children, and was always a special person to our family, so her death was another challenge. We had gone to visit her in Mansfield many times, and the remembrances were rich. She was a seamstress, and even made a special shirt for me when I was about six.

In September, 2001, I began a new phase of working in the church once again. I worked at the Rocky Mountain Conference headquarters building near Iliff School of Theology. My role was "Information Administrator," and I served as a support for the Board of Ordained Ministry and the Director of Connectional Ministry and Assistant to the Bishop. I published a weekly "quick and dirty" newsletter for church leadership in the three-state conference region. This work brought together my ministry commitments and experiences with the technological expertise I had developed over the years. I became the day-to-day communicator through email and web for the conference, under the leadership and guidance of the director of communications. Eventually, I was given responsibility for editing a three or four times a year glossy color publication for folks in the pews about ministries that were happening across the conference. I worked on the website with the coaching of the webmaster. Eventually, I became the web maintenance tech and worked with a designer to roll out a new website based on modern content management technology.

When the conference office moved to new offices in Greenwood Village, I was given an office next to the receptionist and became a frequent host to clergy and laity who came to the office for meetings. Many times, folks would stop and chat before or after their meetings. I valued being hospitable. I continued editing the weekly news sheet and the color bulletin insert, and would serve as backup receptionist, greeting people and answering the phone. I used my familiarity with MySQL, PHP, and web databases to publish a clergy contact database on the web. It was a fun and challenging project. But after I left, the web responsibilities were eventually contracted with a technology company for "mission-driven" non-profits.

I became a go-to person for minor computer and network issues in the office and helped pastors and churches transition to new email processes. At one point, I helped in a refurbishing project that brought free or low-cost computers to churches and pastors. The free ones used the free and open source software Ubuntu Linux operating system that included a free and open source software office suite, web browser, e-mail client, bookkeeping, and Bible study.

I saw my work as one of community-building via electronic means, and when I left that job, I was very happy to hear that many people experienced that through my work. It was truly an honor to serve the people of the conference, just as it had been an honor to work with those involved with MHS and the churches of the parishes I served. I retired from that position in May 2010. I enjoyed my contact with the folks of the conference, as I felt I had found a way to combine my skills for ministry and communications.

One highlight of my time with the Rocky Mountain Conference was a trip to the Sand Creek Massacre National Historical Site as a part of an annual conference session in Pueblo. A caravan of buses took nearly all 600 attendees to the site as part of the exposure to the Methodist role in the massacre. It was a sobering time going through the exhibits and hearing the story of what happened. Bishop Elaine Stanovsky was key in leading our conference in considering this and helping the denomination face up to our role in the racism and genocide that happened in the US and Colorado in the 1800s. The 2016 General Conference featured a report on this. A previous conference had mandated a project to look into the Methodist participation in the events that led to the massacre at Sand Creek in Colorado. The report of this project, *Massacre at Sand Creek: How Methodists Were Involved in an American Tragedy,* was published by historian Gary L. Roberts, who highlighted his findings. With the leadership of Bishop Elaine Stanovsky, former bishop of the Rocky Mountain Conference, a time of recognition and repentance happened at this General Conference.

Another highlight of my conference job was attending my first Western Jurisdiction Conference as a staffer for the conference, supporting the Director of Connectional

Ministries. I got to see the work of the UMC in the whole western region of the USA, which extended from the eastern plains of Colorado, Wyoming, and Montana to the islands of Guam and Saipan!

Activism

In Denver we continued our participation in PFLAG for a time. I also helped form a Bi-Net Denver group that provided support for other people who identified as bisexual and helped PFLAG deal with bisexuality. The group eventually faded—or at least my participation in it did. I continued my advocacy for LGBTQIA+ (Lesbian, Gay, Bisexual, Transgender, Queer, Intersex, Asexual/Allies) inclusion in the UMC in several ways: through the Reconciling Ministries Network; through being a lay member of the annual conference where I and others would produce resolutions encouraging education about LGBTQ persons and a genuine welcome to them; and through the Western Methodist Justice Movement (WMJM). For several years after the Western Jurisdiction's "We Will Not Be Silent" resolution of 2000, we presented resolutions about negative language about LGBTQ persons in the Book of Discipline (the UM Book of Order) and encouraged the study of the issues and welcoming all, including LGBTQ people.

WMJM developed out of the failure of the denomination to alleviate the discriminatory language against LGBTQ people in the Discipline. The 2004 Western Jurisdiction Conference expanded on the original "We Will Not Be Silent" declaration of 2000, and by 2008, the Southern California Methodist Federation for Social Action had arranged a pre-conference gathering of justice-oriented activists to consider what working for justice in the Western Jurisdiction might look like. By 2012, the pre-conference gathering had begun to shape a movement, and the presiding bishop invited the folks gathered to help the Jurisdiction (which has no staff apart from the individual conference staffs) meet the justice and ministry needs of the West. I've been involved since the first gathering in 2008 and have found a place for my advocacy energies for the full inclusion of LGBTQ people in the UMC. As the Western Jurisdiction leadership of the UMC has made it clear that this full inclusion will happen in the West, the WMJM has expanded to include broader concerns, such as the organization style of the Jurisdiction and justice needs in the world. Most recently, we have been encouraging consideration and support of the Christmas Covenant, a plan for the regionalization of the United Methodist Church across the world. This would give the US church a chance to change the judgmental and (in my opinion) ignorant statements about "homosexuality." This developed after the revolt of United Methodists from the punitive stances adopted in 2019 at the Special Called General Conference (see Chapter 10 below on the United Methodist Debate).

As I have mentioned, I have had experience building and maintaining websites over the years. My own, JBenjaminRoe.com, has had a large section documenting the upheaval in the United Methodist Church after the 2019 General Conference and the subsequent rebellion of progressive UMs in the US and Europe.

My final paid work was as an office worker with the Rocky Mountain UM Foundation. I heard about an open position there and decided I wanted to work again, so I applied and worked there about a year doing general office support for the Executive Director and the other office staff. I helped maintain a database and their web site, among my other duties.

SIX

Our Move to Arvada

After Warren UMC closed in 2014, we looked for a new church community. Our criteria were two: that the church be a member of the Reconciling Ministries Network, which meant clearly stating publicly their support of LGBTQ persons, and that it was not small and in decline. We found Arvada UMC, and attended there before deciding to move within a mile of the church (scooter or power chair distance!). We've been welcomed, included and inspired. We've experienced a progressive church that cares about others in service,  learning, and celebrating. Maggie serves as a volunteer congregational care team member. I've served on the personnel committee and the administrative council, and as I outline elsewhere, I've played horn in the various instrumental groups.

So, after 32 years living in a two-story Victorian in the Baker neighborhood of Denver, we moved to Arvada, a suburb

to the northwest of Denver. We found a small ranch house in eastern Arvada, about a mile from the church. When we sold our house in Denver, we had enough money from the sale and a reverse mortgage to adapt the house to be accessible to a scooter and a power wheelchair. Since the first floor is about two steps up from the ground, we had an internal ramp installed in the back sun room. We've been able to add solar power and upgrade the heating and cooling system to a heat pump with high-efficiency gas furnace when needed. The stair glide unit that we had in Denver is now in use to get me to and from the basement without walking. In the basement, I use a three-wheel scooter to get around. The laundry, my office and files, our TV and video center, ham radio gear, and my sizable "junk box" of spare and old hobby parts are also in the basement. It's a comfortable place.

The move was traumatic, with 32 years of stuff that we did pare down somewhat, but we still had a lot of boxes to go through when we arrived in the spring of 2020. A friend of ours who was a home contractor coordinated the move and remodeled the new house to fit our needs: wider doors, an internal ramp, a larger bedroom, etc. He and his wife were a huge help, as was the real estate agent in Arvada who helped us find this home.

During the last week in Denver, I somehow tipped my scooter taking out the trash and hit my head on the pavement. I was out for a bit and ended up in the trauma unit of the hospital with a mild traumatic brain injury (mTBI) with some minor bleeding inside my skull. The recovery from this should have required much rest but was slower because we were in the middle of the move, and also because several weeks after the move, I had surgery to remove a malignant carcinoid tumor. The slow-growing cancer has been contained with some targeted radiation. "You'll probably die with it, not from it," my oncologist said.

This was near the beginning of the pandemic as well, so we had a lot of time isolated in our new home. I spent a lot of time resting and working on little electronic projects and organizing boxes when I had the energy. One of my projects during my recovery from the mTBI was rewiring an old surplus power supply to meet my needs for a supply for an amateur radio transceiver. That involved studying the parts already available for reuse and finding a circuit which would match what was there with what I needed. It was a project I'd wanted to do for years. And I could take it in small chunks at a time. It was some time before I was able to concentrate enough to read beyond a paragraph or two. Gradually, my brain healed enough to read longer articles and even books, such as Daniel Siegel's and Robert Karen's books!

I've enjoyed working on stuff to the degree I know how and have the skills and energy to do.

Friends from church have been super helpful to us during the move and since, too, helping organize the house, hanging artwork from Maggie's dad and other things we've collected over the years, fixing a stubborn door, and changing lightbulbs. These are three of her dad's paintings.

We're enjoying our new life in suburban Arvada, on Quay Street (pronounced "key"—it's a maritime term, meaning a place for loading and unloading cargo).

PART II
MY LIFE: DIVING DEEPER

This section takes a deeper dive into some key events and their profound influences on my life, especially polio and sexuality; my most important accomplishment, Ministry in Human Sexuality; love and marriage; the United Methodist Church debate; music; travels; and finally, conclusions.

SEVEN

Polio: My Personal Disaster

For a two-year-old, especially, polio was a disaster. This is a critical time in the early childhood developmental stages. As I mentioned earlier, the isolation from my parents with only occasional one-hour visits over three months had lifelong consequences.

My earliest conscious memory comes from this time in the first hospitals. I remember being in a ward in a crib, with bars all around. I remember straining to see what was happening way down the aisle at the other end of the room. It was apparently some kind of play, possibly a Thanksgiving one, since I was there over Thanksgiving. There were several people standing up on a slightly raised area, talking to each other. It is in my memory like a "manger scene" or creche. I remember wishing I could be closer and feeling very left out. (It helps to remember that by first or second grade, it was discovered I was very nearsighted, so, of course, I wouldn't have been able to see what was going on at the distance my crib was from the action.)

I remember floating in a large pool of warm water, looking up at the nurse or physical therapist. I have also had the sense that, at some point, I was held by someone, probably a compassionate nurse, who acknowledged my pain and desolation. Having one's experience acknowledged and cared for is a critical part of healing.

I am told that part of the diagnosis of polio was a spinal tap, where a sample of spinal fluid is taken out and analyzed. I am told it is a very painful test since it apparently must be done without anesthetic. I am told it was: I screamed. (I've since learned that the spinal tap was to rule out bacterial meningitis.)

I wrote about some of this experience in a journal entry in 1987. When I awoke that morning, I was shaking in fear, with the vague sensation that I had remembered firsthand some of this.

Remembering and Assessing the Damage

My journey of dealing with this personal disaster for a two-year-old has been a lifelong one. It began with the concern of my parents as I became weaker and weaker with the beginning of the acute stage of polio. It continued with the experience in the hospitals in Little Rock and Denver, and many years later, with post-polio syndrome. The loss of particular muscle function was the least of the impacts. The emotional and psychological impact of the experience wouldn't become clear for years. This is that story.

I know my polio was traumatic for my parents, and probably disturbing for my younger sister, who would have been about a year old. The dynamics when I returned home were probably very different. For one thing, I came "back" to a different home

A Boy Survives

in a different town, since they moved while I was gone. I don't remember anything from those first months, but there are photos of me in a sandbox looking pensive and one of me sitting on the side of a wagon looking solemn. As I have come to understand, I'm sure I was trying "to figure out" what had happened to me, and probably trying to process in a childhood way what I had lost. This process of figuring out what had happened to me continued for years. My assessment has been spread over decades.

In the 1980s, we began to hear about new weaknesses in those who'd had polio years before. I began to understand that my journey with polio was not over.

I was living in Lincoln in 1987 and on a trip to Denver, I visited Children's Hospital in an effort to remember my polio experience. This is where the surgeries took place to correct some of the residual effects of polio and where I had had a couple of other non-polio-related stays (chicken pox for one, believe it or not!).

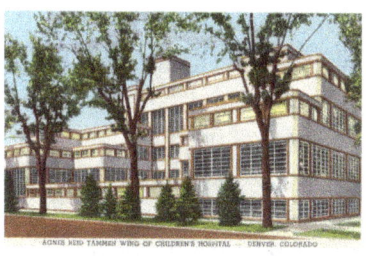

I had driven by Children's Hospital several times over the years whenever I found myself in Denver, but I never thought it important to go inside. That year was different. I knew I had to go inside. I didn't know what I'd find, if anything. I didn't know what I'd remember, if anything.

I drove into Denver from the north, on Downing Street, since I knew that was the street it was on. I drove around to the west, parked, and walked up to an entrance, which one, I don't remember. The old buildings were still there, but it was obvious that the new ones were where the main caregiving for children took place. The old hospital buildings were then apparently mostly offices and labs.

I went in and started wandering toward the older building. I took an elevator up to the top floor, got out, and began walking around the top floor. I remembered one time I was in a sunny top-floor room, probably getting a sample of bone marrow drawn. (This is not a test related to polio; it was likely for that "fever of unknown origin" in my kindergarten year.) I knew it would not be likely I would find this room. I looked out several windows, trying to remember whatever there was to remember. I looked down at what I remembered was the ward where I was at least one time. I wanted to go there, to see what was there now.

I walked through several older halls, with a kind of beige/green tile, some with exposed steam pipes. I remembered seeing these halls from my gurney trips to and from wherever, probably surgery. They had a kind of warmth I hadn't expected. I wandered over to the building in which that ward would have been.

I got the idea that perhaps someone could help me find the place. Suddenly, I thought that maybe there was a chaplain. I would ask. That person and I would at least have something in common, and perhaps they would understand something of what I was seeking.

So, I asked. I found the chaplain's office, with a little difficulty (the hospital Conferences Office didn't know there was one!). I walked in, and met the chaplain, a woman on a residency from the Iliff School of Theology pastoral counseling department. I introduced myself, and we talked a bit. I began to tell her of my desire to make some kind of peace with my childhood experiences. As I talked, all of a sudden, I burst into tears. She was quite concerned, of course, at what must have happened. I hurriedly assured her that the tears were more for the context of the whole experiences, the deep loneliness of not being able to talk to anybody about things, my keeping a kind of detached presence, happy on the outside, very sad and very scared on the inside. I told her of my search for wholeness in my life, my reading, and my interest in therapy, both personally and professionally. She took me around to some of the newer areas, and I could see the very different way children were treated these days, and I felt good about that. I found in her a caring, wise human being, and I gave thanks for having discovered her, by following my inner sense. And I gave thanks for the feelings, through which I rediscovered another part of myself and my life journey. I was glad I went.

As I continued to try to become more aware and understand myself I wrote this poem:

YEARNING

"As a hart longs for a flowing stream..."

My life sometimes seems to be an endless succession of longings—
    for a tricycle,
    a bicycle;
for this telescope
    or that one—or a better one;
for this radio,
    that transmitter;
to be able to make this radio work
    or that one work better;
for this computer,
    that upgrade;
for mom and dad to resolve their difficulties
    to not fight as much
    to understand each other
    to understand me, my uniqueness, my gifts, my needs;
for my loneliness to be seen,
    understood and cared for;
for my grief, my despair, my secret

    to be recognized;
for a space where it all can be acknowledged,
    looked at, dealt with, wrestled with, cried over
        maybe understood,
and integrated.

"... so my heart longs for thee, O God." (Psalm 42)

It was a step towards a deeper acknowledgment of my inner reality. Several years after I wrote that, I was reflecting on my emerging post-polio syndrome in 1991. This story shows a deepening awareness of what the polio experience has meant in my life:

> I was suddenly aware of a sense of dread as I rounded the corner going past Children's Hospital, where I had been as a child for three surgeries. But I wasn't going there. As I signaled to move into the right lane, I was just as suddenly aware of the unmistakable conversation in my head: "But I'm not young and weak anymore. I'm strong and skillful, and I've chosen to come here." I felt my spirits lift. I was going to go to the Polio Clinic at Spalding Rehab Hospital. And I had chosen to go there.

> After changing jobs a few months prior to this visit, I had begun having more trouble with my legs and my back, due to increased walking. I went from a job where I didn't do enough walking and moving around to one where I did too much. I soon found myself wondering what to do. I had seen an article in the Nebraska Polio Survivors Association newsletter on Spalding Rehabilitation Hospital's Polio Clinic. I decided perhaps I would just get an evaluation.

So, I arranged an appointment with Dr. Joan Szynall.

"Now raise your right foot," she said.

I blurted out inside my head, "What? You know I can't do that!"

But of course, she didn't know that. She was, after all, evaluating function. "Now raise your toes." I stared down at the thin, bony, misshapen foot, and felt the tears well up. I decided just to let them come. She patiently waited. No, I couldn't raise my toes, either. The feelings of grief over the lost capability were not surprising, given that I had most likely not been able to adequately express the deep grief at two and a half, when the loss first happened.

I didn't even know what "circuit" to send the instructions through! There was no possibility of a response from these faithful parts of my body. The circuits had not worked for 42 years.

"Well, I'm still alive," I said as I drove away. The words just slipped out unexpectedly. The experience was not entirely unpleasant and provided me with a lot to think about. These seemed to be echoes of an experience long ago from which I was continuing to heal, even as the aftermath was making itself more known.

In this reflection from this vantage point now years later, the "deep grief" referred to was multi-level: it wasn't just the loss of muscle function.

This visit was followed by a series of tests and the diagnosis of late effects of acute poliomyelitis, or post-polio.

In 1993, after I had begun to use a three-wheel scooter, I was beginning to deal more clearly with the experience of the losses from my polio experience. I wrote this:

J. Benjamin Roe, Jr.

ON LOSSES DUE TO POLIO

It's rather amazing to remember I could have climbed that tree
Once upon a time.

I still appreciate the intricacies of trees--
From the ground.

I now get tired just thinking about walking over three blocks,
Much less marching in a parade.

I once was training to be the drum major.
Now I can be my own float.

It's been a long, long time since my body stopped working
For awhile…

They said I wouldn't stand.
The truth was, I couldn't.

And I hurt...
And hurt, and hurt.

Now the body seems to be too quickly diminishing
In stamina and in strength,
As now this leg, then that one
This shoulder muscle, that arm
Twitches and cramps,
Surprised at an unpredicted overexertion.

Once upon a time I was cocky, sure that I had the world
At my beckoning.

The photo shows the spirit,
Laughing, eager and confident.

After weeks of desperate loneliness,
Of unspeakable Secrets, and shattered hope,
Praise for the "good little boy"
Gave birth to
A survival script: pretending.

I kept on pretending, hoping that pretending, I suppose,
Could make it so.

If I were "good enough" maybe it wouldn't hurt.
Maybe "they" wouldn't find out the Secret.
("If you tell, you can't stay," the voice said,
"and your mommy and daddy won't want you.")

So, with no place to go and no way to get there anyway,
the Secret was quietly hidden safely away...
To extract its invisible tribute and subvert
Any hints
To say nothing of progress
Towards its disclosure.

Now the show is no longer possible: sadness comes unbidden
Exploding unexpectedly on some trigger-happy memory.
Hints and teasings, pain and sensations
Creep upon the present-day realities.

Is this "body memory" or is it permanent loss?
Truth will come through experience.

Now pretending is no longer needed.
And Truth will set
The most important "me"
Free.

The puzzle got a bit clearer: there was a "Secret." It added to the feelings of isolation and abandonment with its prohibition of speaking about it.

Another event that helped clarify some of what I experienced when I got polio was this experiment in 2010 of writing a lament as a part of the Bible study *Companions in Christ: The Way of Grace* (2004). I chose to write from the point of view of me as a two-and-a-half-year-old child who had gotten polio. The smell referred to below is the smell of hot wet wool, one of the treatments for the pain of polio. That smell is an instant trigger of memory. From what I know about the warm water tubs and hot wool treatments and the Sister Kinney treatment upon which they are based, this part of my treatment regimen helped the spasms and involuntary muscle contractions that come with acute polio.

A CHILD'S LAMENT

God, you are good.
    You gave me life and fun.
I can run, jump, and laugh.
    You bless me.

I hurt—bad!—all of a sudden!
    Why do I jerk and freeze? Why do I become stiff as a board?
Why does no one know what to do with my screams?
    When will the pain stop?

Please let it stop—now. Please.
    Yet it keeps on and on and on.
The doctors think I should be able to stand up.
    They even think I refuse to stand.

Why can't they see that I can't?

What is happening to me?

My cries bring little relief and I feel like nothing will help.
    No one will help.
Nothing I do, nothing they do takes away the pain.
    It keeps on and on and on.

I smell the smell, I feel the heat.
    It feels good. Pain is less. I can move—a little.

A Boy Survives

I feel the hot water,
    holding me up.

Mommy and daddy have left me here with them.
    Why did they leave me?
Why couldn't they do anything to stop the pain?
    Where did they go?

The time passes so slowly. Day after day they don't come.
    Will they ever come back?

Some of these people are really nice.
    Some are not.
Some are wonderful, loving, warm. Will you be my mommy?
    Some are sneaky and do things to me.

Now I go to a different place. At least there are more
    children here.
    It was good to see mommy and daddy.
Why did they have to go?
    Will I see them again?

Why, God? Why?
    Have you left me, too?
I want to see you again.
    I want to have fun again.
Will I ever have fun again?
    Where did you go?
Is that you in her warmth to me?
    Are you really here?

If I lie still, is that you whispering to me?
    Is it you holding me close?
Is that you down the hall?
    Is that you in the far-off bells?

Please come back and love me again.
> I yearn for that day.

If I ask you to help, will you?
> Please help me get well.

Please help me walk again.
> Please help me run again.

Please let me go back home.
> Please let me see my sister,

My mommy
> My daddy—at home.

The sandbox gives me pleasure.
> I feel the grains in my hands, on my legs.

I see them on my toys.
> I can build things.

I thank you that you are in the sand,
> in the stillness, in the quiet.

I praise you for the sun, the grass,
> the songs of church and the music.

You are my sandbox,
> you hold me in your hands.

You give me life and fun.
> God, you are good.

Thank you.

This proved to be a way to begin to be more in touch with the experience I had as a two-year-old. Painful as it is to write about, a feeling of abandonment becomes clearer in this lament. It is a critical part of my story and development. But also hinted at is a vague memory feeling that somewhere in that whole experience I was being held and comforted, and thus seen and affirmed in the painful reality which was mine during this time, probably an experience that kept a faint glimmer of hope alive.

I was talking with a pastoral counselor at a retreat sometime in the 2010s, telling him of my polio experience as outlined above. He commented, "I can imagine you might have some attachment issues." I bought a couple of books on attachment and found them too emotionally difficult to read, as I began to understand more clearly what had happened to me. However, I continued my commitment to learn and grow from my reading.

Years before, in 1986, in that biographical statement for Clinical Pastoral Education referred to earlier, I had written about a deep sense of loneliness. More recently, in 2022, I ran across the book *Mindsight*, by Daniel Siegel (2010), and decided to work my way through it to see what I could learn about this loneliness. Working with this book, it was rough going in places as I became emotionally more aware of a deep sense of abandonment: after all, I was two years and five months old when I got polio and was in isolation for a month at University Hospital, and then in Children's Hospital for two months, with a visitation policy that allowed only weekly one-hour visits from parents on Sundays. This made it nearly impossible for my parents to visit because this was the day my dad preached at least twice at towns 100 miles away. My dad tried confronting the prevailing visitation practice at that hospital, but was no match for the weight of the institution.

I found Siegel's book very enlightening, helpful, and painful: the resulting heavy emotions and deep sadness and tears were a breakthrough and led to an acknowledgment that I had indeed felt abandoned, and that led to some insight into why I was so distant from my parents. I became more aware than ever before of the source of the loneliness that has dogged me all my life.

I am sure the abandonment I felt in the early hospitals was the major factor in this, especially when I think that I, to some degree, rejected both mom and dad for abandoning me. In fact, psychiatrist and researcher John Bowlby found in his research that children separated from their mothers for a significant time go through three stages: protest, despair, and detachment. (Alsop-Shields, 2001)

Detachment: a consequence of the extended separation from my parents. The thought that "I, to some degree, rejected both mom and dad for abandoning me" at least gave me a sense of agency over something that I had no control over, no say in, and could do nothing about.

I was on my own to figure things out by myself.

Daniel Siegel's book *Mindsight* was successful in reaching me because it was based so clearly on scientific method and research—and thus grabbed the attention of my intellectual curiosity, undercutting my resistance to considering the emotional pain. I decided to buy another of his books, *The Power of Showing Up* (2020), to explore how I was parented. It turns out this was a book about how important attachment is to the development of a healthy self. So, my curiosity led me back to the concept of attachment, the importance of relationships with early caregivers—and the possibility of "earning" attachment in adulthood. This book's focus was on how important it is that parents develop a "coherent narrative" about their own experiences with their parents so that they don't repeat the harm they may have experienced. I found it hard to read as well, but my curiosity had been aroused to reflect further on my experience with my parents. It was a helpful, if somewhat painful, exploration of the relationship I had with my parents. I found a new level of grief at what I had missed.

But also remember that I had two years and five months with my parents before polio struck, time to establish a basic attachment style, which I think may have given me some hope of a better future even as I detached, as well as the supportive touching I referred to earlier. Two years of listening to my dad's preaching and worship leadership probably also gave me an instinct towards hope.

So, this painful detachment further explains my initial emotional resistance to learning about attachment, and perhaps even my difficulty in forming lasting friendships, except with Maggie, my spouse and "best friend forever." I think the consistency of Maggie's caring, sensitive, and empathic presence is what has helped me trust and bond with her over the years we've had together. Outside of this relationship, it's been hard to know how to be a friend.

Yes, it would have been helpful if I'd been able to participate in therapy after polio and the isolation and abandonment I experienced. But who in the late 1940s in Arkansas was advocating for children and would have recognized the issues brought about by the hospital and medical policies isolating children from their families for extended periods of time? That whole experience was abusive, in my opinion.

In fact, psychiatrists and attachment researchers John Bowlby and James Robertson produced a "scientifically impeccable" documentary in 1952 called, *A Two-Year-Old Goes to Hospital*, which was instrumental in changing the way hospitals treated their young children. (Brisch, 2014, 9) That was a bit late for me, but I am very thankful kids are not treated the way I was back in 1948!

There's also the issue of "medical touch," which can be compassionate and warm or cold, dispassionate, and distancing. I don't remember how I was touched during those early experiences, except perhaps the vague memory of being held and comforted, at least once. The hospital record of my initial intake is dispassionate, even cold (for example, "refuses to stand" as opposed to "appears to be unable to stand"). I do remember the care and interest my orthopedic surgeon showed in the three corrective surgeries he did on my left knee and right ankle.

I became aware of faint memories of feelings of desire, wanting closeness, reassurance, to touch and be held by my parents. The memories became clearer, as I got in touch with the deep feelings of abandonment at two-and-a-half years of age.

Another aspect of dealing with disability is learned helplessness, a pattern that was hard to change, and with experience and therapy, I was able to largely overcome it. Learned helplessness is not uncommon for folks who experience a traumatic and/or sustained loss of control, which I did both with the initial infection of polio (no control of parts of my body for sure!) and the hospitalizations and procedures over which I had no control.

As I got more familiar with the realities of polio and its aftermath, I was able to feel less helpless about the state of my body and my internal emotional and intellectual landscape. But this would take some years and therapy work.

Family Complications and Healing

So, my relationship with my parents was a challenge. I was distant from them, largely and initially, I think, because of the detachment that had come from the long period of time in the hospitals without them. And it's possible they may have even distanced from me as a self-protection strategy from their own trauma. My relationship with my mother was enmeshed, which means the personal boundaries between us were not clear, with development as a separate individual discouraged. I think this pattern began before polio, but it became intensified after all the care-giving needed by this new disabled kid. This enmeshment resulted in fairly frequent bursts of disagreement and conflict as I tried to express my individuality. My process of differentiation from her as a separate individual was lengthy, difficult, and "messy," as one therapist called it, commenting that it was usually this way for these types of relationships. Another therapist observed, "You rejected your mother early." It had the ring of truth.

My relationship with my mother was painful, for her and for me. She and I often fought as I was growing up. I experienced her at times as somewhat irrational, it seemed to me. She told me, "You think too much." Letting go of any of us kids was very difficult for her. It seemed she got much of her own sense of self and validation from us kids. My own growth journey, somewhat paradoxically, has been a long and painful process of separating from a person I had rejected but with whom I was enmeshed. I can only speculate about what suffering, abuse, or trauma she may have experienced that led to the symptoms I witnessed and dealt with. It was never a conversation we could have had. This could explain, at least in part, however, her lifelong interest and advocacy for the less privileged and marginalized.

When I left for college, I was relieved to be away from the painful dynamics at home, and I took advantage of living away from home to withdraw from the rest of the family to enough of a degree that my sister Phyllis complained after my dad's death that I had "abdicated" my "older brother" place in the family, so that she felt like she needed to pick up the slack in dealing with my mom. Her disappointment and resentment were a natural human reaction, but hard for me to hear about. For me, it was a survival mechanism.

As I've said, dad and I were distant emotionally. I've wondered if another early decision of mine may have contributed to this distance: according to my parents, I would ask "why" of him a lot. I wonder if I withdrew from him when he could not tell me "why." He was a minister, after all... It never occurred to me that he might not know, or did not know. I think saying "I don't know" was hard for him, and it might have been hard for me to hear if he had said it!

Some of the grief at dad's death was indeed a lot of grief over what might have been. He and I, for a number of reasons, just never seemed to connect very well. We were different, of course, with different interests and experiences. As I have reviewed what I knew and remembered of his life, I know we tried at various times. He listened non-judgmentally to my faith questions and gave me a couple of very helpful books, both by Leslie Weatherhead, *The Will of God* and *The Christian Agnostic*. He affirmed my questions and encouraged me (and his parishioners) to think and to ask questions. He did seem to see and affirm my interest in science: I think either he or he and mom gave me books, such as a large picture book of astronomy that I loved, and others like *The Boy Scientist* and *The Boy Mechanic*. Interestingly, I liked the *Scientist* one better than the *Mechanic* one. I think, in these ways, dad supported my development as an individual person.

Some of my sadness, even before he died, was over not really having him the way I wanted to. But he was a good pastor and, as so often happens, somewhat better outside the family than in it. At my urging, he even arranged to have a sexuality education program available in the Ainsworth church when I was in high school.

Being a "preacher's kid" made the abandonment and the attachment issues harder. The Methodist (now United Methodist) denomination assigned pastors to local churches, now usually upon consultation with them (less so in 1946 in Arkansas). This system expected families to cut all ties with friends in the old town when they moved to a new one. That expectation has softened somewhat for children of pastors, but, for me, that pattern fit into my relationship difficulties from abandonment, detachment, and enmeshment, and meant that I didn't make friends easily. Years later, one of my childhood friends got in touch with me, and over lunch, mentioned his hurt that I "just disappeared."

My sister Phyllis and her husband Michael introduced me to two major resources for my attempt to understand myself: Alice Miller and Ken Wilber. Swiss psychiatrist Alice Miller's books, especially *The Drama of the Gifted Child*, *Thou*

Shalt Not Be Aware, and *For Your Own Good,* were helpful in validating and deepening my understanding of my experiences of giftedness, as well as sexual and physical abuse. American philosopher and writer on transpersonal psychology Ken Wilber's *Transformations of Consciousness* (co-author, 1986) helped me identify and trust my journey. In a sense, Wilber's explanations helped me gain a kind of "roadmap" to my developmental journey. It was reassuring to be able to identify the "lesion" in my development that the polio experience caused, and, of course, it is related to the attachment issue. I also found my reading of psychiatrist James Masterson's book *The Real Self* (1988) helpful as I tried to figure out how to discover and heal my sense of self.

I identify with the sentiment in a story about Alice Miller's son Martin, a psychotherapist who has written about his life with his mother. He writes about his ambivalence towards his famous mother from whom he suffered a great deal, but who gave him the information he needed to survive.

In a later interview, he indicates how he now feels free, but also is aware of what he lost (Sela, 2014). This is similar to my experience in writing this book.

My own parents were wonderful in the commitment they made to treat me like "any other child," and not dwell on my lessened physical abilities. They encouraged my interest in technical things like steam engines, and later astronomy and radio. They were wonderful in their commitment to the importance of education, spiritual growth, and justice-seeking. But the tensions between them referenced here were troublesome and helped keep me distant from them. Thus, the paradox: enmeshed (with mom) but distant. I am convinced that my distance from my mother in particular is what kept me from descending into greater pathology. It was a survival strategy. The pathology I think I avoided was a destructive and active rebellious "acting out" on the one hand and a suicidal despair on the other (though I did have a couple of occasions when this latter response was briefly considered, and wisely decided against).

So, I grew up not trusting adults much. I think this primarily was due to the detachment from caregivers I experienced in the hospitals early on, as I've mentioned. And I saw frequent bickering, mutual accusations, criticisms, and arguments of my parents. I saw them talking to each other in less respectful tones. It was not good modeling, and was confusing. I sometimes felt like I was in between them.

One of the commands from my mother (I don't think I ever heard it from my dad) was "Don't ever talk about what happens in this house to others. You could hurt your father's career." I heard this most strongly after I told her in eighth grade that I had confided in a caring and compassionate campus minister at a youth event about the problems I saw in my parents and their relationship. When I told my mom about this, she angrily told me not only should I not have done that, but I was never to talk to anyone outside the family about them. Obviously, this was not something I could talk with her about (nor dad). This left me isolated again with nowhere to turn, except to wait, since I had decided running away was not wise. It was years before I really trusted any other adult in authority.

There was one time in my high school years after mom's older brother had committed suicide that she agreed to go to a psychiatrist (in Omaha: far away). It helped, apparently, but when he started to focus on their relationship, she stopped it. (I do think dad understood better than I thought he did about what was going on, but his commitment was to the marriage and us kids, so he hung in.)

Learning that mom had stopped the Omaha therapy sent me into one of the lowest times in my high school years, and I thought about running away. I decided, however, it would be foolish and would be roughly equivalent to jumping from the frying pan into the fire: I didn't know enough, didn't have enough experience to survive on my own at that point, and that while I had a vision of a better life for myself down the road a few years, I would commit myself to waiting and learning all I could about life and prepare for a good job that would give me the freedom to go on my own path. So, I stayed and redoubled my efforts to accomplish as much as I could. This is at least part of the motivation to be so active in high school activities.

I had a similar moment in college when I actually did disappear from campus for 24 hours and came to a similar decision: that a better future was ahead, and I could keep going towards whatever it might look like.

My CPE autobiography referenced my desires to escape, or transcend, a painful childhood. For most of my life, music, astronomy, radio, science, and religion were ways I sought to deal with (and, to a degree, avoid) this pain of my early years. But these areas and interests were also an expression of my individuality, my gifts and graces, part of my development of a separate self, my own person. And this is all a spiritual part of my life that prods me, guides me, and is constantly there with me as I journey through it all. So, it wasn't all just "pretending" or an attempt to escape.

Music has been critically important in my life and survival. It was something that came somewhat naturally. In music was expressed profound emotions beyond any words: joy, tragedy, yearning, playfulness, freedom. Music was also an inspiration to me, from the great hymns of the church to the great symphonies. And by listening, singing, and playing, I could participate in soul-soaring, transcendent freedom. I could also establish for myself a sense of my competence in something that was truly mine. In high school, I developed a nightly schedule of listening to far-off classical radio concerts on such stations as WGN in Chicago, KSL in Salt Lake City, and occasionally WLW in Cincinnati. Music still lifts me out of myself and gives me perspective on what is happening inside me and around me. It is an important component of my survival mechanism.

As I've mentioned, in fifth and sixth grades, I became a star gazer and with dad's help, made that reflector telescope. I could see detail on the moon and far away objects. Contemplating and seeing the vastness of the universe gave me a perspective on my life. Seeing the Andromeda galaxy has been a favorite for years.

In eighth grade with my first amateur radio license, I reached northwestern South Dakota on my first contact, and both coasts and Canada by the time I advanced to the next license. In high school, I became active in the message-handling aspect of ham radio, eventually becoming the "net" manager for the Morse code network in Nebraska. I thus escaped into the airwaves, finding some companionship, more competence, and independence.

I think my exposure to the Methodist way of grace through my dad and others along the way gave me hope that "it gets better," even though I sometimes didn't know exactly what that "better" might look like.

It has been the promise of hope and of a better future, of fulfillment, and of God's presence that has kept me going, sometimes barely, throughout the years. In fact, in an article in the Washington Post on March 30, 2023, by columnist Amanda Ripley, I discovered that in some of my darkest days of high school and college, I had applied these principles (however imperfectly) to the decisions I made:

> Hope is more like a muscle than an emotion. It's a cognitive skill, one that helps people reject the status quo and visualize a better way. If it were an equation, it would look something like: hope = goals + road map + willpower. "Hope is the belief that your future can be brighter and better than your past and that

you actually have a role to play in making it better," according to Casey Gwinn and Chan Hellman in their book, *Hope Rising* (2018).

To put it directly, while believing that somehow in my future I'd find a better and more satisfying life, I decided to do what I could to survive and make a better life for myself. My "roadmap" at those times was school, a satisfying job, and marriage.

Counseling and Therapy Experiences

In seminary, because I had had contact with pastoral counseling faculty, I began to be able to tentatively trust counselors. So, at one point when we needed a bit of assistance in our marriage relationship, Maggie and I went to couples counseling in Claremont. It was, in fact, my first "real" counseling experience. It helped us communicate better and got us over a hump in our relationship.

Besides couples counseling in Claremont and Omaha, and the supervision I received in CPE and as a counselor myself, I have participated in several therapy experiences. I was finally able to carefully trust certain professional counselors and therapists. One especially productive time was with a psychologist in Lincoln during a crisis time. He used a dynamic psychotherapy modality, which helped me connect my present behavior and thought patterns to experiences early in my life. He was able to help me build a stronger sense of self and confidence as an individual. He was insightful, a careful listener, empathetic, and appropriately challenging at times. It was a productive, fruitful relationship.

The thoughts of philosopher and developmental theorist Ken Wilber gave me a rough map of my journey and thus more confidence to explore. It has also been the use of a spiritual direction process based on the psychosynthesis practice of

Italian psychiatrist Roberto Assagioli that has given me an emotional sense of God's love and presence that I had never had before. And it has been the support of this process that allowed me to go deeply into my grief over all the childhood losses, a griefwork I am able to do because of new tools of understanding and self-awareness.

It was in Lincoln in the 80s when I had a series of very enlightening sessions with spiritual directors who worked with the techniques of Assagioli. Re-reading my journal entries from that period has been very enlightening. I see I identified abandonment back then, but it appears I was defending against the depths of that acknowledgment, likely because I didn't feel safe enough. (My work was unstable financially, and I was working with some challenging clients.)

Then, when we moved to Denver, I was able to work with a pastoral counselor who could work in several modalities, including EMDR (Eye Movement Desensitization and Reprocessing), which helped give me access to more of the traumas of my childhood. Another person I worked with was a professor of pastoral counseling at Iliff. This experience was very meaningful and helpful in gaining insight into how my present-day issues were connected to events that shaped me in much earlier life. One thing he asked me as it appeared that I would lose my AAPC membership was, did I have a ministry to the church? That insightful question helped me see that that has been true of me for a long time, as I have advocated for the full inclusion of LGBTQ people in the UMC. It has continued even after I surrendered my UMC ministerial credentials.

It is interesting to me as I reread some journal entries from that period that I admitted not wanting to know what happened to me. I was thus repeating my mom's lifelong pattern of repression and resistance to acknowledging the unpleasantness and trauma of some life experiences. As I mentioned above, Daniel Siegel's book and my work with it was another important breakthrough in my willingness and ability to face the realities of my early life with some tools with which to do so. Also helpful was another pastoral counselor who used Cognitive Behavioral Therapy and taught me ways to change less helpful thought patterns and habits, a skill I continue to use.

EIGHT

Sexuality: The Puzzle

I have had a life-long fascination, curiosity, and wonderment about sexuality, originating at least in part from an experience in the hospital. Unfortunately, talking about sex was just not done openly and honestly in my earlier years, and not just in my family, but in the larger society as well. So, if I had questions, there was no one who was safe to talk with about the puzzle.

Pleasure and/or Abuse?
It was in the 80s when I began to suspect that I had had some kind of early sexual experience as a very young child, perhaps in a hospital with polio or chicken pox—it was very unclear.

In therapy, I became aware of the repressed memory of someone stimulating my penis with the words, "Here, let me make you feel good." In the context of the devastation of polio, the isolation, loneliness, and abandonment feelings, anything that provided some pleasure would have felt pretty good. Certainly, it was inappropriate, but should I call it abuse in this context? Any more than the hospital policy of weekly, one-hour visits from mothers and fathers? This policy is clearly child abuse, in my opinion. Both experiences have had lifelong consequences. There was cruelty in the treatment of many children who were hospitalized especially in the 1940s and '50s with polio; my experience was apparently mild in comparison to that of many others. Bruno (2002, 60ff.) gives voice to some of those who experienced this.

Unfortunately, there's more to this early sexual experience that further exacerbated the isolation, because there was a vaguely remembered command that went with it, which surfaced some years later: "You can't tell anyone," the voice said, "and your mommy and daddy won't want you." This spoken message is what made it, without a doubt, abusive. The isolation and abandonment were sealed. While this stimulation was a pleasurable experience and was probably one of the few enjoyable moments of the polio hospitalization, the "secret" made it abusive and more damaging to my relationship with my parents and my development of trust. And it fit into the rules in my family of not talking about sex and guarding the privacy of the family. This experience, along with the attitude in culture and home that we didn't talk about sexuality, led me to be really curious to figure out the puzzle: "Why? Why is something that feels good so wrong?"

While it is commonplace that, by definition, sexual contact by an adult with a child is harmful and abusive on its face because a child, by definition, cannot give informed consent, we know that some mothers (or grandmothers) would sometimes stimulate the genitals of a very young child as a way to comfort and calm them, perhaps to get a diaper changed. Is this abuse?

The central issue in all of this is consent and the development of a child's decision-making ability: Most societies set the age of consent to be 16 or later. But kids start making decisions much earlier: Do I want chocolate or vanilla ice cream? Do I play inside or outside? And how many children would consent to corporal punishment? At what age do we have to be so we are able to foresee the long-term consequences of any decision? What does consent mean? Is consent simply yes or no, or is it "enthusiastic yes" or emphatic no? My guiding principle is that "no" or "not yet" or "not now" or "no more" is always an option, no matter where one is in a behavior, including sexual intercourse.

Note my decision at two and a half to reject my parents. As I said, this was a decision I made, perhaps as a way of taking back some control for myself in the context of being utterly at the mercy of my caregivers, but I could not have known the complicated and lasting consequences of that decision. I'm still working on how the situation that led to that decision has shaped my life and later decisions. This is true of many decisions over the span of our lives, not just for immature children in an overwhelming situation.

Remember my question at age five about whether Jesus had been real and my decision that it must be so and the subsequent decision to join the church when I was twelve. Were those decisions invalid because of my age?

This is a hugely controversial area, both in the field of childhood sexuality and theological ethical thought. My purpose here is not to debate or review the literature. My bibliography appendix contains references to resources on the issue. Actually scientifically studying children's sexuality and children's sexual experiences (often labeled abuse) is very difficult, from a legal, ethical, and societal point of view. The level of emotional reaction to the subject makes it even more difficult to study objectively. My own journey of introspection and therapy has helped me understand better and come to a feeling of greater peace with all these issues.

Why?

Another piece of the puzzle came when I was probably about four. We were living in Bayard, and my sister and I were in the bathtub. Mom was giving us our customary baths together. I somehow noticed that my sister was different from me, and probably asked my usual question: "Why?" The verbal answer, if it was even said, was not memorable. But it was the last time we took baths together.

One of my memories is of being told fairly frequently as a toddler "Don't play with yourself." Never mind that pediatrics and science today knows that self-pleasuring is common in children, even occurring in utero! Oh, and why limit that to genital touch? After all, we encourage playing with toes and fingers. Exploration of one's body is an information-seeking activity, is it not?

An incident that powerfully remained with me is also brief: I was probably six, and we were visiting my aunt's house in Arkansas. I made the mistake of coming down from my nap and into the kitchen where mom, her sister, and my grandmother were having afternoon coffee—with my hand in my pants. What a storm! "Don't touch yourself down there!" All kinds of comments about politeness and what I was learning were made to my mother, and to me. So that gave me more to wonder about.

But there were positive experiences that helped. One real gift my dad gave me in junior high was during a tearful conversation I had with him about masturbation. I was doing it and feeling very guilty and uncertain about it. As I've said, we didn't talk about sex in our household, so this was a very hard conversation to have. He listened with care and compassion and provided a helpful perspective. I have continued to enjoy it ever since, even more so as I've gotten older.

I think I was in sixth grade when I got "the speech" about sex and how important it was to wait until marriage. Around this time, I was given Evelyn Millis Duval's book *Facts of Life and Love for Teenagers,* which did help some. I had the sense, though not the actual words, that "sex is dirty," and "save it for someone you love"—a common double message (the phrase is from sex educator Sol Gordon).

In high school, I heard about the sexuality education program called "Sex and the Whole Person" from the Methodist Church, and convinced my dad to arrange to have it for us kids. It was led by the couple who were the youth leaders, and though I don't remember much about the class itself, I know it helped.

This class helped lift the veil of secrecy and open a door of understanding. But I long wanted to heal, from whatever happened to me in the hospitals and what was happening in my family. Having someone I could confide in would have helped me deal with the issues I've outlined, but there was no one until much later. The detachment and the sexual contact and the abusive message that accompanied it in the hospital set up the loneliness and difficulty in trusting anyone enough to confide in and talk to.

My mom angrily forbidding me to talk about the family outside the family added to my teen distrust of adults, which lasted into late seminary, when events forced me to confide in my advisor that I would not likely graduate on time, as I have mentioned.

I would occasionally talk a bit with my college "dorm mother." After college and seminary, I eventually began to learn through psychotherapy and spiritual direction to be free of the nearly chronic depression of my adolescence and young adulthood. There were times when I tried to reach out and find help in understanding and working out problems and issues I could barely articulate. I was most aware of parental unhappiness and bickering, though I was unsure what it was all about. I was unsure of career directions, unsure of myself, unsure of my self-worth.

There were times in college when I would get very depressed, and feel more isolated than ever, and more than once in high school and college I briefly considered an early end to my life.

But I always knew there was more, and that, with patience, I could find it, though I had no idea how.

Clarity

Clarity about these issues of sexuality as they were related to my experience, questions, and decisions began to emerge in seminary. There, I had opportunities to be in small group counseling with spouses, and I remember this as helpful, at least reducing my anxiety about the counseling process. Maggie and I joined a gestalt group offered by faculty member Frank Kimper. We also worked a few sessions as a couple with him and went for marriage counseling a few times with a therapy couple at a Family Service affiliate. I consciously chose not to go too deep in those few opportunities in which I participated, because I was afraid of what might come up (yes, I even consciously thought that!). But, the short experience with the family counseling center was helpful in our relationship, and helped me think maybe I could handle more.

It was during the last year in my first appointment in southeast Nebraska when the sexuality puzzle got more complicated. In the summer of 1977, we went to visit a male seminary friend with whom we had grown close. We had gone to the UCLA bookstore, where I had bought Don Clark's book, *Loving Someone Gay* (1972). On the way home on the plane, I was reading it. He has a rather broad definition of "homosexuality," and I suddenly became aware that I fit his definition! This sudden realization and clarity of my same-gender attractions led to a personal crisis. I was feeling confused and afraid. "Homosexuality" was "incompatible with Christian teaching," my church denomination said, so my ministry status could be at risk. I shared my feelings with Maggie within the first week after I had recognized them. Her immediate response was, "Do you still love me? Do you still want to have sex with me? Do you want to still live with me?" My answer was an immediate and enthusiastic "yes!" Her response was, "Then let's work it out." I've written more about this coming out process in an appendix.

Also in the fall of 1977, an evaluation of my performance as a small group facilitator on a church sexuality education program team added to this crisis. I participated in an initial career evaluation interview at Menninger's in Topeka that resulted in a psychiatric referral to Lincoln. I went for a couple of sessions and decided to look elsewhere for the help I felt I desperately needed. While his initial comments (you're "driving with the brakes on") were useful, he wasn't a good match and his focus was not on the area I felt an urgency to address: my confusion and anxiety about my sexual orientation. The career assessment would have to wait a bit.

I continued looking for a counselor who could help me sort out my confusion and anxiety. I had been involved in a new sexuality education ministry in the Nebraska Conference, the Conference Human Sexuality Division of the Board of Discipleship. Around one of the meetings I confided with a colleague who suggested I visit a psychologist in Omaha who was United Methodist and who had done some sexuality consultation with the church. Through him, we were referred to a couples therapy team, Ellie and Les. They were a godsend. They primarily worked with a combination of transactional analysis and psychodynamic modalities. One of the issues we worked on was the pattern I was doing that I had seen in my father's way of talking with my mom in a critical, impatient, and belittling way. It took willpower, a commitment to change, and some work over a number of years to change that pattern. We worked for several years with this couple: driving two and a half hours from Endicott to Omaha in the afternoon, having one session, then spending the night, doing homework, and having a morning session before returning back to the parish by noon. (My senior pastor had said that my day off could only be 24 hours.)

A Boy Survives

Sometime during this period, I found the UM gay caucus group, Gay United Methodists, and was invited to attend a meeting in Dayton, Ohio, to meet other folks who had attractions to same-gender people. I went in the spring of 1978 or 1979 and was impressed with the folks I met. They were clearly committed to supporting each other and others who could not be there, and to changing the church's stance, even though it seemed very unlikely. I got to meet Michael Collins, a young gay UM minister and pioneer in the movement, who was an encouragement to me on my journey. However, when I happened to mention in the group that I was bisexual, the immediate response was, "Bisexuality is not our agenda." I had not been aware of the discussions and tensions in the New York City groups between gay men, lesbians, and bisexual people, so I walked into that naively! Well, bisexuality wasn't really my agenda, either: It was finding folks who would understand my attractions to other men, and who shared my faith. So, I kept quiet and didn't use that term the rest of the meeting, nor any of the other meetings until several years later.

The paranoia back then was really high. After all, you could lose your job, your family, your support system, your career, and maybe even your life if you were found out. In some parts of the US and the world, this danger still exists. Suspicion was high when Maggie attended a meeting in Indianapolis with me the following year: was she a spy from the Good News organization (a conservative UM group)?

I was deeply affected by the story told by a young associate minister at one meeting. While he was away, the SPRC (HR committee) found out he was gay, changed the locks on the parsonage, and tossed his belongings out on the front lawn for him to discover when he got home. He was not given another appointment. Hearing his pain, heartbreak, and devastation at having been outed and then ousted from his ministry made a huge impression on me. I was to hear stories like that for the next 40 years. Wesley's rule, "Do no harm," was ignored when it came to dealing with us. It is still not honored even today, at least in some parts of the denomination.

I was given a copy of Blair Blurbs, the newsletter published by the United Methodist Gay Caucus for the 1976 General Conference, and learned about John Wesley's ministry with Mr. Blair, a young man in prison in England for being gay, and the flack he took from his fellow Holy Club members. I learned about those courageous leaders who were at the founding meeting of the United Methodist Gay Caucus in 1975. The meeting in Dayton followed up on a meeting in Dallas to change the name to Affirmation: United Methodists for Lesbian/Gay Concerns and to incorporate in Texas. I heard about Gene Leggett who'd been suspended from his ministry, and Paul Abels, one of the first openly gay pastors in the UMC and pastor of Washington Square Church in New York City.

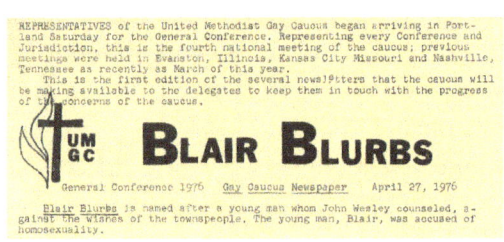

In fact, in 1980, a sexuality committee of the Rocky Mountain Conference sponsored a conference on homosexuality in Denver that featured Paul Abels preaching. We drove from Lincoln, Nebraska, to attend and met some wonderful folks. In all these experiences and many more over the years, I grew more certain that the stance of the UMC, that "homosexuality" was "incompatible with Christian teaching," was just plain wrong, and that I should be involved in changing the culture of the church and of society to be more knowledgeable, more understanding, and more compassionate about the range of sexual orientation.

The solution I ultimately found to all this was to found Ministry in Human Sexuality to address the silence, the prejudice, and the fears associated with sexuality.

NINE

Ministry in Human Sexuality

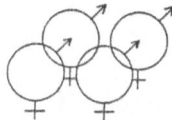

MINISTRY IN HUMAN SEXUALITY
J. Benjamin Roe, D.Min.
P. O. Box 80122 Lincoln, NE 68501
(402) 476-9913

I consider Ministry in Human Sexuality (MHS) my most important achievement. The origin of the idea for a "ministry in human sexuality" came from these experiences and my career assessment process. These all clarified that I wanted to address the silence and lack of knowledge about sexuality in the UMC and in the culture. It was a huge learning experience. One of the most important things I learned was that I'm not an entrepreneur.

MHS started in the fall of 1980 with an advisory board and a single room office in the educational wing of Trinity UMC in Lincoln. MHS was incorporated in February, 1981. In August 1982, we moved to the Anderson Building, an old office building downtown. It was a comfortable space. It had a public restroom that had some rather explicit graffiti, which gave me a chuckle and which I photographed as some local gay art! I'm sure it's long gone by now. In April 1984, we moved to the Lincoln Center for Community Services Building, across the street from Pershing Auditorium, where the 1964 MSM conference had been held. This building contained a number of non-profit community service agencies.

The mission statement I developed for MHS was "Affirming the Gift of Sexuality: Toward Whole Persons, Growing Relationships, Inclusive Community" and expanded that to:

- to acknowledge, proclaim, and celebrate the gift of human sexuality;
- to bring good news about the gift of sexuality to the human pain, brokenness, and estrangement surrounding many areas of human sexuality;
- to enable and encourage persons to increase their understandings and skills in expressing and embodying love and compassion.

I explained this mission as one of witness, service, and support. MHS gave witness to the gift of sexuality. MHS served those who wanted help in understanding, appreciating, and growing in their sexuality as a gift, an important and valuable part of personhood and wholeness as individuals, in relationships with others, and in spirituality. MHS sought to support those who are in "exile" because of misunderstandings about sexuality.

MHS became a 501c3 non-profit agency and provided pastoral counseling with a sexuality and relationship emphasis, education on sexuality matters, and advocacy for more inclusion of those who experienced disability, or who were gay, lesbian, bisexual, and transgender persons in church and community. I wrote a number of articles for the singles newspaper and worked with two other agencies on sexuality and disability workshops presented in several communities around Lincoln. I learned about advisory and governing boards, fundraising, policy setting, supervision, and certification. I led many educational workshops and presentations on topics such as sexual orientation, homophobia, mixed-orientation marriages, disability and sexuality, spirituality and sexuality, and holistic health and sexuality. I was part of a group of four human service professionals who presented a process we developed for caregivers on disability and sexuality to the annual Building Family Strengths symposium in 1982. I wrote and presented a paper and a panel on mixed-orientation marriages to that symposium in 1985.

We were contracted by the United Methodist Nebraska Conference to develop a task force to plan a conference for 1982 on a positive and affirming ministry with homosexual persons. It was called "Counseling Homosexual Persons" and was held in April. It was a positive approach that affirmed the gay and lesbian people and their families who were trying to learn about this part of sexuality that had attracted such strong and condemning feelings.

Out of this grew a proposal for an ecumenical group to provide more conferences like this. So MHS facilitated the formation of a "Joint Strategy and Action Team" (JSAT) of Interchurch Ministries of Nebraska (IMN) on "Ministry with Homosexual Persons and their Families." These IMN teams were always multi-denominational. This one had several denominations participating, including United Methodist. The JSAT hosted two conferences on Ministry with Homosexual Persons. The first conference, entitled "Affirming the Wholeness of Community: Homosexuality, Families, and the Christian Journey," featured Dr. David Switzer, professor of pastoral care and counseling at Perkins School of Theology and co-author of *Parents of the Homosexual*. It was held in Kearney and Omaha, Nebraska, in 1983. A second conference was held in 1986 in Lincoln at the Unitarian Church, and featured Bishop Melvin Wheatley, an outspoken voice for full inclusion in the United Methodist Church in the 1970s and 1980s.

We were active participants in the American Red Cross AIDS Education Committee (statewide), the Lincoln-Lancaster

County Health Department AIDS Committee, and the Nebraska Health Department Consensus Conference on long-range planning for AIDS. Other activities included participation in the Gay/Lesbian Information and Support Line (GLIS), and Parents and Friends of Lesbians and Gays (PFLAG).

I advocated for increased acknowledgment and appreciation of lesbian, gay, bisexual, and trans persons in the church and in the culture. MHS was a support for the formation of the GLIS Line and for a foundation that tried to get a return engagement of the San Francisco Gay Men's Chorus after their first concert in Lincoln in 1981.

In 1982, the Lincoln City Council was considering putting to a popular vote the issue of including gay and lesbian people in the protected classes of the city's civil rights provisions. I and the MHS board decided to testify in support of this measure, encouraging society to be inclusive of gay/lesbian people.

Counseling clients began in February 1981, and through 1988, over 300 clients were served, including individuals and couples. Counseling concerns included issues such as sexual orientation, understanding sexuality and spirituality, enhancing sexual expression, sexual abuse and incest, improving communication in relationships, and disability. Part of the approach to counseling was a commitment to transparency and clarity of expectations. This led to a counseling services brochure which let clients know that the counseling model used was based on a growth, wellness, and empowerment model, rather than a more traditional medical model.

In a parish pastor's life, counseling parishioners is nearly always short-term, issue-oriented, and usually faith-oriented. But in the life of a pastoral counseling professional, the issues are sometimes short-term and sometimes longer-term, dealing with deeper issues of relationship dysfunction and its roots, with grief, with self-esteem and self-knowledge and insight, and with guilt and anxiety.

My experience with Ministry in Human Sexuality included all the above. Though direct counseling about the specifics of sexual expression was a part of my work, knowledge of relationship dynamics and communication, the knowledge of human personality and the practice of psychotherapy were also very important. The broad definition of sexuality that undergirded my work meant that much of what I dealt with had a sexuality dimension to it. As James B. Nelson, author of *Embodiment: An Approach to Sexuality and Christian Theology* (1978), put it: "Sexuality is a sign, a symbol, and a means of our call to communication and communion."

Developing a supervision policy and supervision agreement was an important part of my learning about what providing counseling was all about. One of the most meaningful experiences, besides the clients and their stories, was the supervision of my work with them with some very good counseling supervisors, who helped me understand important, helpful, and useful concepts. I learned a lot, and took several psychology classes at the University of Nebraska. I began the process of membership in the American Association of Pastoral Counselors (AAPC). This involved supervision by AAPC and would lead to pastoral counselor-in-training membership.

Questions were asked regularly about why I did what I did in sexuality ministry and my decision to found Ministry in Human Sexuality. I had several reasons, some of which were very personal.

The first reason I usually gave was that there was a need. Sex was not talked about when I was growing up, and it still was not talked about much when I began Ministry in Human Sexuality in 1980. When I was young, I often wondered why there was such a big deal about this one area of life, why this subject was not mentioned in some places, why one talked so carefully about it when one did talk.

So there was a need for someone who could talk openly and teach and provide programs about this troublesome area of life, for any group that desires it, and in counseling for those who can talk to no one else about some of their deepest and most embarrassing issues. Hopefully, there would be less trouble and more understanding and light shone in the darkness through my ministry in this area.

Second, there was a theological need. I recognized that there was, and continues to be, a long history of ambivalence about sexuality within the Christian tradition, ambivalence that is not a necessary part of the tradition, in my opinion. There is a need for responsible reflection and study of human sexuality informed by faith. I saw myself as being able to assist in this reflection. My seminary experience and my professional project on theology and sexuality education gave me a good place from which to start in this theological reflection.

Third, there were, and still are, needs of women in a sexist society, and of sexual minorities: developmentally challenged, differently-abled, gay, lesbian, bisexual, trans, queer, intersex, and asexual people—the spectrum of human sexuality. Each group has its own story of faith, how their social status has caused them problems, and how they have come to see their spirituality as a result of their experiences with sexuality.

Fourth, there were more personal experiences with my own physical disability and sexual orientation. I have felt feelings of diminishment, of lowered worth on the dating "market," a lessened ability to compete in the usual ways for males in our culture. I have felt fear in acknowledging my attraction for other males, without diminished attraction to females: the uncertainties about that, the risk of talking about it because of church rules, the feelings of isolation in dealing with it, the identification with others who shared a problematic sexuality, especially gay and lesbian folk. I have experienced the importance of community in the midst of my initial coming out bi, and my continuing attractions to individuals regardless of their gender, orientation, or presentation. I have and continue to experience the presence of God's grace in the midst of my doubt and fear, and a stronger relationship with God as a result of my search and God's patience.

If I could help others with their questions and their development of faith, I wanted to do so. As a child, I was not able to help my mother get the help she needed with the issues she had; now as an adult counselor, I could help folks who wanted to grow. And in the process, I also gained greater understanding into myself.

My Decision to Leave MHS

My dad's death in 1987 helped me clarify through my grieving the reality that I was not going to make a living at Ministry in Human Sexuality, Inc. As I've said, I'm not an entrepreneur and provided too much service without adequate fundraising.

I had told my clients for some time what I had been taught and what I had learned for myself through experience: go through the pain of grief and let it teach you, go through it and learn what you need to know. So, when he died on March 30, 1987, I promised myself to go through the grief process intentionally and find out what was there for me through it.

My experience was instructive. I had begun awareness of my grieving before dad died—he had not really been available to me emotionally, a truth I had only recently acknowledged. I had grieved the loss of something I had only gradually begun to understand: the loneliness, the lost closeness, and a lost happiness. I finally had begun to feel, truly feel, the deep sadness of my childhood, the source of the depression that had dogged me most of my life.

I felt many mixed feelings. I felt a new appreciation for dad's solid commitment to doing what needed to be done in his profession, even when he didn't feel like doing it. I felt a new appreciation for the many people dad touched. And I felt envy at what he had meant to others, and at what I felt I had missed. I felt a lot of sadness.

Most of all, I felt a deep, draining sense of loss and emptiness—my legs didn't want to move, my arms just wanted to dangle down by my side. My body felt like lead. I was numb. I watched myself, I felt, I listened. I did some guided imagery spiritual direction. And I felt some of the zeal to change the world leave me—I had not changed my family, I had not changed my relationship with either mom or dad. I could not bring my parents back nor could I bring back anything else of what I had lost. I could not change death. I could not change the past. It was gone.

I read *The Drama of the Gifted Child* (Miller, 1981). I read *Life Is Goodbye, Life Is Hello* (Bozarth, 1985). I acknowledged the feelings that came up. I began to get a clearer sense of what I could not do. I found myself acknowledging more clearly what was really true about my life, my family, myself, my work. And the financial pressure helped me acknowledge what I had known for some time: financially, I was not going to make a living at MHS, and I did not now have the energy to do what was needed to turn it around, if that were even possible. I reflected a lot. I began to change a core belief that I could "control through weakness" to "I can influence." I let go of my need for grandiose schemes and recognition. I began to recognize dimly that perhaps MHS had been, in some small way, a way to substitute for, or maybe try to get some recognition from him (symbolically) while keeping it from coming at the same time—after all, sexuality work was not an area that was highly recognized or appreciated in our family. I don't believe he and I ever really talked about the sexuality ministry itself.

The final gathering of board and friends in celebration of the seven years of the ministry was a bitter sweet time for me. One friend commented that I didn't seem to be totally present—I suppose that's no surprise. Kinda numb. The grief process has taken years.

Another friend had made a rather thick scrapbook of memories of the events over the years. I think it is an appropriate memorial. I think MHS did a lot of good during its seven-year life, and helped move the awareness of the diversity and reality of human sexuality further along, especially for the LGBTQ community.

Even after I left MHS, however, I continued my advocacy for LGBTQIA+ people in the UMC, from our new home in Colorado. I supported the Reconciling Congregation Program (now Reconciling Ministries Network) and was their volunteer webmaster for a short time. I participated in advocacy work to try to move the UM General Conference to be more welcoming to LGBTQIA+ persons. And I've participated in the organization of the Western Methodist Justice Movement since its inception.

TEN

The United Methodist Debate

There is much written about the development of support for the LGBTQIA+ community in the USA and in the United Methodist Church over the decades. I won't attempt to summarize it here; Bishop Karen Oliveto's book, *Our Strangely Warmed Hearts* (2018), covers it very well.

The United Methodist Church's debate at the General Conference in 1972 ended by turning a pastoral statement on human sexuality into one that was judgmental and condemning to "homosexuality." During the debate on the paragraph dealing with sexuality, held during the closing hours of the Conference, it was decided that the practice of "homosexuality" was "incompatible with Christian teaching." Every General Conference since then has debated that phrase, most of the time heatedly. In 1984, they even added that no "self-avowed practicing" gay person could be ordained or appointed and that no same-gender marriage ceremonies could be held in a UM church, nor could any UM clergy officiate at a same-gender marriage ceremony.

A Boy Survives

At first, I wasn't tuned into the controversy as it applied to gay people (using the generic term in use at the time). However, I was well aware by the time I was in seminary that the larger church was sadly conflicted about human sexuality in general and how people dealt with their sexuality. My papers and professional project, besides their purpose personally to try to "figure out" what sexuality was all about, were my attempt to critique and hopefully provide a better perspective for the church.

The addition of the discriminatory words, that "homosexuality" is "incompatible with Christian teaching," has done a lot of damage since 1972. Obviously, this was the cause of my fear and panic in 1977 when I realized that I, too, had significant same-gender attractions. Besides this very personal connection, from my studies of sexuality, I knew that this attitude towards LGBTQIA+ people was against what science was learning about the complexity of sexuality, sexual differentiation and development, and sexual orientation. (As a result, I've also begun to put the word "homosexuality" in quotes, since it is now clearly an out-moded term and doesn't acknowledge the complexity of human sexuality.) This stance was also against the doctrines of grace that John Wesley emphasized in the founding of the Methodist movement. So, it became a justice issue for me as well.

Over the years since my coming out, Maggie and I have been involved in the movement for full inclusion of LGBTQIA+ people in the UMC, including in leadership positions as clergy. We've been involved with Affirmation: United Methodists for LGBTQ People and our Allies and the Reconciling Congregation Program (RCP) of Affirmation and then its spin-off to the separate organization, the Reconciling Ministries Network. We were active in a Boulder-based Affirmation group for several years. We've attended several General Conferences where the church "law" is debated and decided.

The 1996 General Conference was held in Denver, and we were involved in planning the witness of the RCP at that conference called "Open the Doors." Part of the witness was a musical, written by Jean Hodges, a Boulder teacher and Affirmation member, and Julian Rush, a talented musician and composer, and one of the first openly gay ministers in the UMC. It was called "Come to the Table" and was performed several times for attendees at the conference to get a gay-positive view of the issue of coming out and inclusion. This conference did not change any of the negative laws against LGBT people.

We also went to the 2000 GC in Cleveland, where one of the LOVE sculptures is located. We were again involved in the organizing and support of the movement for inclusion. We decided to participate in a floor demonstration during the conference, and the catcalls, yelling, and meanness of the words coming from the delegates as we walked onto the floor made a lasting impression—in fact, it was a traumatic experience. We weren't among those arrested, but there were arrests made outside the hall as well. All in all, it was a very discouraging, even traumatic, experience.

Then in July of 2000, we heard that the Western Jurisdiction Conference, meeting in Casper, Wyoming, had made a statement entitled, "We Will Not Be Silent." They declared that in light of the harm that was done by actions of the 2000 GC, "The votes may have been cast but our voices will not be silent." It was a striking and prophetic witness. When we heard about this, we just had to drive to Casper to be with these people who were speaking out so strongly and prophetically— and in our part of the UMC here in the West! It was exciting. It turns out this proclamation was a turning point in the Western Jurisdiction.

We went to the 2008 and 2012 General Conferences in Fort Worth and Tampa. In Tampa, I was managing editor of the Love Your Neighbor Coalition daily newspaper, a full-size ("broadsheet") eight-page publication. No change in the exclusionary language happened. I was proud of my work with the staff of the paper and managing some of the significant articles we published.

At the 2016 General Conference in Portland, things did not improve. The progressive organizing was even stronger. I had agreed to provide my writing skills to Affirmation for the Love Your Neighbor Coalition and wrote short articles for the publication of the coalition, including "What Do We Know About Sexuality?" and "Sexuality and Spirituality." Some of the conference delegates nearly came to blows over the issue, until the conference asked the bishops to lead us out of the impasse. It was a critical time and much has been written about all this. The outcome of this watershed conference was the formation of a Way Forward Commission that came up with a proposed way to settle the issue.

The special General Conference in St. Louis in February 2019 of all the official delegates from all the annual conferences of the worldwide UMC was to have settled things, but it didn't. In raucous and contentious debate, it continued the discriminatory language against LGBTQ persons and relationships, and added punitive measures. That broke the impasse in a sense, with many individuals, pastors, churches, conferences, jurisdictions, and even bishops speaking out against this result. In fact, several bishops, including all in the Western Jurisdiction, pledged not to forward any complaints they got against clergy for being LGBTQ or for performing weddings or covenant services for same-gender couples.

I became excited at reading about the rebellion in the US church, but also in Europe. I began to collect all the statements and news stories I could find on my personal website, JBenjaminRoe.com. For a time, the United Methodist Association of Retired Clergy posted a link to my collection. It also helped me clarify my faith commitments, which are on my website and in an appendix.

I don't fully understand why, but I felt on the edge/fringes of that conference, not fully connected with the activists like I used to be. It may have been related to the gradual realization that I couldn't take much more disappointment—I think I've been hurt, even traumatized, by all the negative stuff I've heard and experienced over the years, and just don't want to deal with the rabid anti-gay, anti-sex, misogynistic stuff anymore. There is also the fact that getting my scooter to an accessible part of the venue was a hassle, and further set me apart. In fact, one aspect of this is that the rabid irrational stuff triggers my feelings of helplessness to make a difference with my mother. Now, I will try to settle for influencing.

I learned through all these experiences the importance of the perspective of faith and spiritual life, the importance of human persons, of listening carefully, of tact and graceful suggestions, of writing, public speaking, teaching, community building, workshop leadership and training, and the importance of collaborative leadership styles.

My website, JBenjaminRoe.com, also contains many resources about sexuality, from papers, presentations, speeches, bibliographies, and articles. There's even my seminary Doctor of Ministry (D.Min.) professional project, comparing and contrasting two sex education programs for the church, in the context of a theological discussion from the point of view of Reinhold Niebuhr's writings.

Can the UMC survive? Yes, I have been seeing it move into a new life. We are healing. The disaffected and, to my mind, those who can't or won't deal with the complexity of sexuality are leaving, and a "rebirth of passion" for our historical ministry of personal spiritual development and social justice in the UMC has re-emerged, as was clear in the General Conference held in Charlotte, North Carolina, in 2024. In a way, I think the denomination has gone through a process like what a gay person goes through in coming out: the suppression of the full expression of our sexuality before finally accepting the reality of our lives. This General Conference repealed all of the restrictive laws put in place in 2019, and removed all of the harmful language about LGBTQIA+ sexuality from our Book of Discipline, including bans on ordination, same-gender marriage and services, and church funding for any education about the complexity of sexuality that includes positive references to LGBTQIA realities and persons. Much more on this Conference can be seen at this link: UMCGC.org and JbenjaminRoe.com/gc2024.

ELEVEN

Friendship, Love, and Marriage

In grade school, I had crushes on a couple of my classmates, and enjoyed May Day when I would take a May Basket and try to run to "avoid" a kiss. The "May Day" tradition when I was in grade school in Big Springs was that classmates would take a small basket of treats and leave it on the doorstep of someone they liked, ring the doorbell, and then run. The game was to get caught and kissed. So maybe I shouldn't have run so fast… I never pursued friendships with the girls, partly because I was encouraged by mom not to get involved with girls; I had the sense that it was risky behavior (it wasn't until later that I understood the "dangers" of sex). So a "safe" significant friend was TJ, whom I referred to earlier, a male friend whom I liked and spent time with.

In high school, I was attracted to several girls, though they were always "already taken," so to speak. From this vantage point today, I think I knew my attractions were not only to girls. I think this is an important reason I kept a distance from my classmates and didn't socialize much. There was no safe way I could get close to anyone, even though I might be attracted to them. Adolescent sexuality, particularly related to same-gender attractions, is a challenge. I've talked about this part of my life in the "sexuality" section above. Given my family dynamics and my detachment from my parents during my polio treatment, I also didn't really know how to make friends, partly because there was always this sexual dynamic on my part that I didn't know how to handle.

As I mentioned above, the summer after my sophomore year, I attended camp at the Methodist Camp Fontanelle near Fremont, and met a girl from a small town in northeast Nebraska. I invited her to the Junior-Senior Prom. The evening was awkward, as I described earlier.

I've described some of my dating experiences during my first year and into my second year of college. Mary and Maggie were my first serious dating experiences. I learned a lot about attractions, intimacy, communication, and my own values as I navigated the choices involved: into which relationship I would put my most serious energy.

Maggie tells when she first noticed me walking across the Nebraska Wesleyan campus with my characteristic bouncy walk—in fact, my nickname with my small circle of friends was "bouncy." She asked a friend who that was, since she somehow intuited that this person would be an important person in her life. "That's my brother Ben," my sister Phyllis told her. In fact, Maggie's dorm counselor was Bill's girlfriend Diane, whom I later discovered had been engaged to Bill at the time of the play!

After some indecision on my part, I eventually decided that Maggie and I were the most compatible together. We continued to date during the remainder of our time at Wesleyan and enjoyed each other's company in the various activities we did together. Wesleyan had curfews for women: nine p.m. for freshmen and 10 p.m. for sophomores. Maggie's dad was a Methodist minister, and when he became a superintendent of the Lincoln district, she lived at home her third and fourth years, in the Lincoln District parsonage across the street from First UMC and Nebraska Wesleyan. How convenient! After I delivered her home after a date, we often would go into the basement for special quiet time together.

We graduated together in May 1969, got married on June 8, 1969, and moved to Claremont, California, where I was to attend the School of Theology at Claremont, and into student housing at the seminary. All in the space of several weeks. No stress!

The marriage service at Lincoln's First United Methodist Church was traditional, set as a worship service. My dad's church members in Elmwood and anyone in Maggie's dad's district were invited. Our fathers officiated, with Maggie's dad delivering the homily. First UMC's pastor C. Ebb Munden was our pre-marital counselor. A musician friend played Jeremiah Clark's trumpet tune for the entrance, a superb vocal music student performed a solo of I Corinthians 13, and another music student played the large organ at First UMC. Maggie's grandfather Carl McGlasson, in his late 90s, wanted to participate by "giving her away," so when that question came, he said loudly, "I do!" The reception line was a bit of an ordeal: my smile felt pasted on by the end!

We had put the car into Maggie's parents' garage across the street from First UMC. It was a disappointment to my groomsmen, who admitted they looked for it with a stack of Playboy centerfolds they had intended to plaster on it!

We retrieved the car and took off for Omaha, where we spent our first night together. That in itself was an experience, marked by the fact that across the hall from our door was the ice machine! Nearly all night long folks were coming to get ice...

We spent the next few days at Ponca State Park in a cabin, where Maggie baked a cake in a skillet. (She's continued this creativity.) The rest of the meals were not memorable, but that was fine with us! We were in love, after all! The last night, we spent in a tent in the Park, since the cabin hadn't been available for the number of days we wanted. That was another thing that made the honeymoon memorable. Tent camping, however, we did again only once or twice more in seminary with friends.

So, our adventure as a married couple began. In the next week or so we started off for Claremont pulling a small U-Haul trailer with our 1964 Chrysler Newport. The tunnels weren't finished under the Continental Divide, so we made our way over Loveland Pass. We passed through Bryce and Zion National Parks on the way to California, past the Mohave Desert, and to Cajon Pass above San Bernardino. Our first glimpse of Southern California was as we came down through Cajon Pass into the rather thick smog of the valley. We made our way through it on historic Route 66 called Foothills Blvd. to Claremont. We lived in student housing until we moved to

an apartment in Los Angeles about a block from First Baptist Church, where I had a student internship.

For Maggie's birthday on our first year there, I gave her a puppy: a German shepherd, husky, and beagle mix that was adorable! We called her Sandy. She went with us everywhere, including a trip to San Francisco and to Portland to visit Maggie's family.

When we moved back to the Claremont area after my internship months at First Baptist in LA during the last semester of my second year of seminary, we lived with another couple for a school year, then moved to Upland to a small house in the middle of an orange grove. We lived there until we moved to the La Cienega neighborhood of LA itself, just off Interstate 10, the "Santa Monica Freeway," where we lived while Maggie attended the UCLA graduate school of Library and Information Science and I worked at Theta Cable Television in Santa Monica part time. The La Cienega neighborhood was racially mixed; we lived in a duplex with a tiny yard for our dog Sandy to do her bio necessity. We took her everywhere we could, leaving her in the car with the windows rolled down (which wasn't the best, but given how close we were to the sea, the temperatures weren't high during the day). It was a bit better than leaving her at home to bark frequently.

We both graduated in June 1975: Maggie with a master of library and information science degree from UCLA and me with a doctor of ministry degree from the School of Theology at Claremont (now called Claremont School of Theology). We had experienced culture shock going to Southern California. Now when we moved back to rural southeast Nebraska, it was culture shock coming back!

We were there in Jefferson County Nebraska three years and then moved to Lincoln in 1978 to a rented home near 59th and Glade Streets. It had a nice backyard with a weeping willow tree, and it was in this yard that we celebrated our 10th anniversary of marriage with a small group of friends. It was a recommitment service officiated by two women clergy we had very much appreciated: Rev. Susan Davies and Rev. Elizabeth Beems. We had worked for over a year and a half on our marriage relationship and had renegotiated a lot of our understandings and wanted to celebrate that with our friends. It was quite a contrast to the very traditional service we had had 10 years before at First United Methodist. We wrote our own vows. This time, they were based on the experiences of dealing with some special friendships over the first 10 years and my coming out as bisexual, as well as the counseling we were participating in at that time. These were the vows we wanted to recommit to by then, shared with our friends. We exchanged new silver rings that were a unique matrix of open spaces. 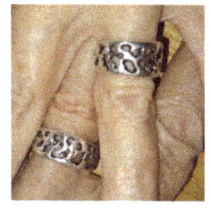 The company that made them still specializes in "unique and funky custom jewelry," which these rings certainly were. We still wear them.

By then, we had expanded our ideas of "fidelity," to mean our commitment to each other's growth, development and full personhood as we were growing together and in our partnership in exploring life. It no longer meant sexual exclusivity. Over the years, we've each had some special and meaningful friendships in addition to each other. They have enriched and strengthened our life together. We found the book *Open Marriage, a New Life Style for Couples* (O'Neil and O'Neil, 1972) helpful in reflecting on and constructing our marriage style. Some of my readers may remember the early seventies were a time of questioning even whether marriage was worth "saving." In its chapters on negotiating our agreements, open and honest communication, role flexibility, equality, trust, and jealousy, we found much for enriching communication and decisions about what our marriage would be like.

I've mentioned elsewhere our therapy experiences in Omaha, which was a huge benefit and put us on a track to continue our growth in intimacy and communication. Over the next decade, we also participated in Marriage Encounter and Marriage Enrichment programs. We have valued our individuality from the start, and we chuckled when someone at Marriage Encounter remarked we seemed more like "married singles." Because we valued our individuality together, we took that as a compliment! But in retrospect, now knowing the emotional detachment I experienced in the hospital, that comment makes a bit more sense.

We worked together, helping to establish or strengthen LGBTQ-related projects. We did some presentations together through Ministry in Human Sexuality and the UM Affirmation caucus. We worked together in the sexuality education experiences that the conference Committee on Human Identity and Relationships offered for teens. Maggie was part of the team that worked with the older adult groups. We were involved in some AIDS-related activities: we attended a UM-sponsored conference in San Francisco and encouraged Don Holloway, the founder of a Boulder-based organization, "AIDS, Medicine and Miracles." And we have both been involved in Affirmation: United Methodists for LGBT Concerns over the years. Maggie served on the National Council during the time when the Reconciling Congregation Program became its own organization, separate from Affirmation, now the Reconciling Ministries Network. We almost always attended national convocations of RCP/RMN and national meetings of Affirmation together.

As we've pieced together jobs and careers, we've each been support for each other. Maggie was consistently my support all these years. I've kept home fires burning when she would work with Bread for the World, initially in Washington, D.C., and then as a Western US organizer in Denver. And we nearly always talked on the phone when she was away, often as long as an hour each night! These calls kept the relationship flowing and growing.

Maggie's experience being with a special friend as he died from AIDS led her to consider hospice ministry, and to enroll in Iliff School of Theology. She graduated in 1999 with a master of divinity degree and started a nine-year hospice chaplaincy ministry with the Hospice of Metro Denver (now The Denver Hospice). Since then, she has served FEMA as a chaplain to staff, and as voluntary agency liaison for several disasters. Her final chaplaincy was with Lutheran Medical Center and Collier Hospice. She retired in 2020 and continues serving as a volunteer care team member at Arvada UMC.

Maggie is a companion, friend, fellow searcher and explorer. She is intuitive, sensitive, patient and assertive. With her I have learned the disciplines of relationship: communication, constructive conflict resolution, and the forms of intimacy. Our life together has been one of mutual support, encouragement, and growth. We share much together: interests, commitments, and dreams, especially regarding feminist spirituality, affirmation of the diversity of sexual orientation, and holistic views of sexuality. We are also very  much individuals and sometimes have needed intentionally to schedule time together. I appreciate her sensitivity, depth of spirituality, courage, love of life and adventure, and her willingness to explore life and relationship.

We decided in 1978 to remain childfree. The motivation for my part of the decision was not something I'm particularly proud of, but I just didn't want to subject my child(ren) to the possible harm that I experienced as a young person that could come from my mom's moods and criticisms. I felt it would also complicate my relationship with my mom in a harmful way, for her and for me—to say nothing for Maggie. We weren't stable financially, either, with me just ending my first ministry position and not knowing what was next. For Maggie's part, she couldn't honestly think how to juggle a career and a family, so we decided she would have a tubal ligation. Here's an interesting story about that: several years ago, we were in the ER for something related to Maggie, and the woman physician found that out and was saying how we should have gone for a vasectomy, since they are "easily reversed"—something we didn't know in 1979. But it's apparently not as easy as she made it out to be. Anyway, this conversation was uncomfortable for us since we didn't want to go into it with her at all. With a couple of knowing glances, we negotiated the decision to say very little in response.

Over the years, I've had significant and meaningful friendships with several gay and bi men who have helped me adjust to my new reality and provided some needed support and companionship.

TWELVE

Music and Its Place in My Life

Music is an important—indeed, critical—part of my mental and spiritual health. Whenever I get "off center" or out of sorts, it's usually orchestral, "classical" music that helps me reground myself and lift me beyond the present to the more transcendent.

When we moved to Big Springs, my parents got my sister Phyllis and me into piano lessons with Miss Riss when we were in third and fourth grades. Playing and practicing wasn't something I remember fondly—it was often more of a chore. I didn't like to practice and really wasn't very good at playing. However, the experience gave me a really good start with learning the keyboard, reading music, hearing the pitches and associating them with specific notes on the page and on the keyboard. It's not what is called "perfect pitch" but close enough to sing and eventually play the "French" horn (professionals just call it the horn). In fact, when I practiced at home, I would sit on the piano bench so I could play the note and then match it on the horn. I still visualize the keyboard when I play the horn, which enables me to transpose hymns from the hymnal.

So, I started music when I was in grade school. Music class helped develop my singing. I had a good soprano voice and was dismayed when, one day in sixth grade, my voice cracked and my pitch fell by at least an octave! I became a bass. Eventually, I enjoyed it and learned to pick out the bass pitch from the chords I heard.

This ability came in handy when I started learning the horn in sixth grade. In fifth grade, I started on glockenspiel and the snare drum, and for a few weeks, I even had a trap set in the parsonage in Big Springs, playing along with band music I heard on the North Platte radio station, KJLT. I remember being thrilled to play the glockenspiel on the "Great Gate of Kiev" piece by Mussorgsky. Still love that piece. But my music teacher, Mr. Stacy, noticed I had a good sense of pitch and he said he thought I would make a good French horn player. I took lessons from him and used a school horn (throughout all my school years, including seminary).

Big Springs had a community concert series that we went to as often as we could. One of the concerts featured a soloist who was playing the horn, the instrument I had just started learning. I wanted to hear how someone who played it well sounded. I was very disappointed when an asthma attack kept me home.

When we moved to Ainsworth, I enjoyed singing bass in the church choir. I played in the school band on second horn for a couple of years, and then first horn my last two or three years.

Band was a really fine experience under Mr. Thomala and Mr. Stanek. We played music that was a mix of popular music, marches, and classical. In fact, in eighth grade, I believe it was, I was playing second horn and worked very hard learning the triple-tonguing that is required at the end of the finale to

Dvorak's New World Symphony. It was a thrilling experience to play this piece. It's still one of my favorites.

In high school, I participated in various instrumental contests, playing horn solos and getting good reviews. I even played for church on several occasions. I got to play in the Nebraska All-State Band as a sophomore in 1962 and two honor bands at Hastings College in '63 and '64, my junior and senior years. These were highly rewarding experiences. I remember going up to the conductor after one performance and apologizing for missing a note in one exposed place. He was gracious and said he'd heard professionals miss notes like that. That was a note of grace and encouragement. Two pieces that I appreciate and that take me back there are Mussorgsky's prelude to his opera, Kovantschina, and Wagner's Rienzi overture.

I also enjoyed singing bass in the high school chorus, though instrumental performance was much more interesting and fun.

When I went to college at Nebraska Wesleyan, I had never played in an orchestra before—I had always played in a band. But someone had told me that the orchestra needed horns. I had enjoyed playing the horn since sixth grade. I had gotten fairly good, and had done well in high school, so I thought I might have a good chance to get in, maybe as second or third horn.

So, I tried out. I don't remember the exercises or the pieces used for the try-out. It was probably something I had prepared, and some sight-reading. I do remember being completely intimidated by nearly everybody at college. I had come from a small town of 2,000, a small high school graduating class of 73 or so, but we did have a good band, and I had worked hard at playing first chair, first horn for my last years of high school. I also remember being sure that there were folks who played horn, probably from the larger schools, who could play better, and who I'd be playing with in both band and orchestra. I had already begun band, and landed second or third horn.

I was totally floored when I found out that not only had I made the orchestra, but I had also made first chair, first horn! That was fun. One of the pieces I enjoyed playing was Jacques Ibert's "The Birds" which has bird calls of various kinds and led one student to remark that Jacques had a brother named "Smoke." ("Ibert" is pronounced ee-bare. Remember the Forest Service campaign, "Only you can prevent forest fires." And who was speaking on those signs?)

I loved it. I knew I could play, but I had no idea that I played that well. I knew there was more to learn, that we could always play better, that there was always somebody better. I was always so conscious of my mistakes, my fluffs, my faults. My mom had made them quite obvious whenever she heard me—she focused on them, possibly because of her own inner critical voice, a common trait in those who've experienced their own early trauma and tragedy. So I had decided in high school that her word didn't mean much when it came to horn playing, but that practice of always looking for the mistakes, the problems, the places for improvement, was pervasive and took its toll on me (it wasn't only horn playing that was affected by this mindset!).

I played in orchestra for several years, playing for concerts and for opera *(Camelot* and *Faust)*. My happiest moments were playing the classics with the orchestra, mastering (well, almost) the difficult parts, and singing my soul out in wordless ways.

The band, under the direction of Mr. Marshall, once did a tour of towns in northern Illinois. Besides enjoying playing and traveling, I remember sitting way up in a balcony at Orchestra Hall for a Chicago Symphony concert. I played first horn in the band in my final year, and performed a solo at a concert on campus.

After graduating from Nebraska Wesleyan and starting at the School of Theology at Claremont, I was asked to play in the orchestra that accompanied the high church celebrations during the year: All Saints, Lessons and Carols, and Easter.

At the celebrations the chorale sang, and sometimes I sang with it. Always there were the instruments—it was glorious! There were strings, trumpets, oboe, horn, trombone. I played the horn, and learned to transpose directly from the hymnal. I loved it. My lip was in nearly top shape, so I could play the high notes. I remember these times as some of my most inspirational. I felt like my soul soared.

("Transposing" was a challenge because the horn's native pitch and printed music clef are not based on middle C like the piano, but on F: i.e., a horn may play its "middle C," but it sounds an F on the piano.)

When I served the Jefferson County Larger Parish in Nebraska, I played horn for church in Fairbury and Endicott a couple of times. In fact, in Fairbury, an older gentleman who was the director of a community band years earlier sold me an old horn (from Czechoslovakia!) for 50 dollars. I played that single horn until 2019, when I bought a double horn (these have capability to play in the key of B flat, an interval of a fourth higher than the normal horn in F, making high notes easier to play accurately). I forgot how much heavier these horns are than a "single" horn, so I had to improvise a horn holder.

When we lived in Lincoln in the 80s, I got to play in a community orchestra and go on a short tour in a town a couple of hours from Lincoln. We played Dvorak's cello concerto and Mendelssohn's *Reformation Symphony,* still two of my favorites, and another high point in my horn-playing. Arvada UMC has had cantatas and a Christmas orchestra, every year except during the COVID-19 pandemic, in which I enjoyed playing. After the pandemic wound down with vaccinations and lower case counts in Jefferson County, AUMC again had an instrumental ensemble that usually played on fifth Sundays. Besides performing, I love listening to music. And, in fact, there's a power of live music that isn't the same as music played loud on home stereos! So we have been season ticket-holders of the Colorado Symphony for years. Arvada UMC hosts musical performance groups, like the Jefferson Community Band, St. Martin's Chamber Choir, among others.

During the COVID-19 pandemic, the Colorado Symphony had to curtail their concerts, so we signed up for the Berlin Philharmonic's Digital Concert Hall. That was not the same as an in-person concert, but this orchestra is probably the best in the world, at least according to John Williams, who conducted a wonderful concert with them in 2021. I enjoy especially watching moments with the horn players.

I have had lots of wonderful experiences, both playing in bands and orchestras and listening to the horns in other concerts over the years. I find I listen for the "inner voices" of harmony in particular, probably because of my experience playing in those voices.

THIRTEEN

Travel Highlights

Over the years, we've enjoyed traveling, usually to a church-related function of one kind or another. These trips have been part of what has helped us stay United Methodist in the midst of official policies that were not welcoming to openly LGBTQ persons.

We've attended most annual conference sessions in the regions we've lived: Nebraska and Mountain Sky (Colorado, Wyoming, Utah, Montana). In Nebraska, annual conference usually met at Nebraska Wesleyan and First UMC in Lincoln. The more memorable annual conference sessions include the ones where my sister and I were ordained in 1976 and when I was formally approved to found Ministry in Human Sexuality in 1981.

The Rocky Mountain Conference session was held for years in Fort Collins at Colorado State University. I usually worked up a petition calling for greater acceptance of LGBTQ persons in the church. We went to Salt Lake City after the

2002 Olympics. I was conference staff for this one, supporting the Director of Mission and Ministry Ron Hodges. That year was significant because it was the first conference held outside of Colorado in years.

The 2019 conference was held in Billings, Montana, and was a positive, celebrative time. We elected progressive delegates to the General Conference in 2020 (which didn't happen because of COVID-19 and was ultimately delayed until 2024!). A highlight was during the lengthy ballot counting, where Bishop Karen played the percussion trap set on stage while people danced!

The 2022 conference was held in Helena, Montana, and happened to be right before the wedding of Maggie's grand-niece and her wife on San Juan Island in Washington State, so we drove first to Helena and then on to Friday Harbor on San Juan Island. We wanted to visit Glacier National Park, but the timing wasn't right: we could only get to the visitor center; the road through the park was not open yet because of snow. The wedding was beautiful, as was most of the scenery getting there, but when we tried to board the ferry afterwards, the car right ahead of us was the last to board, so we spent the night in the parking lot of the ferry! Sunrise was nice. This was one of the longest car trips we've done together. We were careful to trade off driving frequently. I don't think I'd do a car trip like that again.

As newly-weds, after our honeymoon trip to Omaha and Ponca State Park, our marriage started off with driving to Claremont in 1969, pulling a U-Haul over Loveland Pass. It was a leisurely and inspiring trip. We stopped at Bryce and Zion National Parks for brief sight-seeing. Those parks are awesome, and we went back again some years later for longer visits.

On the occasion of Maggie's sister Jeanne's fiftieth wedding anniversary in Tucson over the Fourth of July, we started out in our Honda minivan. We were shocked by a sudden collision with a deer that had decided to cross Interstate 70 near Rifle, Colorado. It was night by then, and we didn't see him until he crashed into the front of the car and windshield. The Honda was totaled. We ended up riding Amtrak back to Denver, renting an accessible van, and starting over. We enjoyed visits to Bryce, Zion, and Grand Canyon National Parks. These provided reflection on how brief our time is as human beings on this earth. On our way through Flagstaff, we visited Lowell Observatory, the observatory that had been used in the discovery of Pluto in the 1920s. I got the T-shirt.

Driving through Phoenix on the way to Tucson, I was shocked to see the external temperature reach 110 degrees! Wow. The time in Tucson was not that uncomfortable, since everyone had air conditioning, and the fireworks were in the evening. One highlight was visiting one of their friends in the community who had a large telescope, and who showed us Saturn and its rings. The skies were almost as clear as they had been in Big Springs in my childhood.

In the 80s, we attended many of the national gatherings of Affirmation, beginning with my first one in Dayton, as I've mentioned before. These meetings were in many locations in the US and helped us stay United Methodist even when officially it wasn't so welcoming.

Over the years, we've attended most of the convocations of the Reconciling Ministries Network, from Washington, D.C., to San Francisco, Denton, Texas, Estes Park, San Antonio, and Charlotte. Again, these have provided inspiration to hang in with the activism to make the UMC a truly inclusive church.

One of the most significant was the very first one: We drove from Lincoln to the convocation of the Reconciling Congregation Program of Affirmation in Chicago in 1987 in a snow-storm! We vividly remember driving through Iowa in a blizzard with a heater that quit east of Omaha. Maggie suggested using a hair dryer. So, we found a JCPenney store in

Des Moines and bought a cheap hair dryer which I rigged up to the cigarette lighter, which gave just enough heat to keep a small section of the windshield clear. But we were warmed and inspired by the gathering of like-minded folks who knew the issues and had our shared commitment to making the church a more inclusive and loving place.

We marched in the 1993 March on Washington for Lesbian, Gay, and Bi Equal Rights and Liberation with Affirmation: United Methodists for Lesbian and Gay Concerns (bi hadn't been added yet). This was also the time of an Affirmation meeting, where I had helped arrange a series of presentations on the topic of bisexuality. At the parade, the usual religious hecklers were along the route, and we all sang "Jesus Loves Me, This I Know" as we passed them. We also got applause for representing a church group. It was a very special time for us, being in the company of so many out, joyous, and proud LGBTQ folks.

We usually traveled by air with United—until they left me in one of their wheelchairs for an hour without returning my scooter. Frontier was next, until they didn't trust my word that the batteries were truly non-spillable and made me take it apart to show them the markings on the batteries. Southwest has been the best so far, treating my disability status matter-of-factly, but even they did minor damage to my scooter on a trip to Newark. But I do enjoy the perspective of seeing the earth from 35,000 feet!

Speaking of Newark, in the 2000s, I served on the Affirmation National Council for three years and traveled to meetings in Newark, Indianapolis, and St. Louis. On the Newark trip, I was able to use public transit; in Indianapolis, I used Yellow Cab's accessible cab service and had a delightful time with the veteran driver.

In the most recent 2023 Convocation in Charlotte, NC, we celebrated 40 years of the Reconciling movement in the UMC.

It was wonderful to see and celebrate with both old-timers like us and younger activists and others who wanted to witness to the gift of being queer Christians. One of many highlights was to hear retired Asbury seminary professor Steve Harper speak and dialogue with Bishop Karen Oliveto. One wag called them "the odd couple." We got to help celebrate the part that two early pioneers played in the Reconciling Congregation Program, Mark Bowman and Beth Richardson. The trip itself was pretty uneventful, with Maggie using a three-wheel scooter for the first time. This was the first time I'd flown since before 2019, and I was using a power wheelchair. I bought a foldable power chair because I didn't trust the airport handling of my big power chair. This turned out to be a good decision because it enabled us to ride an accessible cab together in both Charlotte and in Washington, D.C. where we went the next week.

We had planned to do sightseeing in D.C., but came down with COVID-19 and ended up spending a week in isolation in a hotel in D.C., not far from the White House. All the tours and museum reservations were canceled. I did a wheelchair tour of the area between the hotel and the Washington Monument on the last day, taking lots of photos. Unfortunately, the plan to take the Metro train to the airport didn't go well because of my difficulties with a small elevator that trapped me inside before I could get both suitcases inside. The one that got left behind unattended was gone by the time I was able to get back to pick

it up. It had both chair battery chargers in it, which was the most significant loss, besides the suitcase itself. I blessed it to whomever picked it up, assuming it wasn't the security folks at the Washington Metro (it was never recovered).

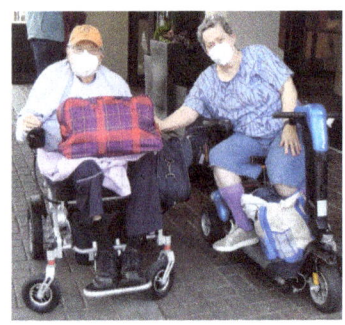

Our activism has taken us to a number of General Conferences over the years, all of which were disappointing from the point of view of trying to change the negative official stance of the UMC towards LGBTQ persons. But each trip was enjoyable in that we got to keep connected with other activists.

I once traveled to Tijuana to visit a friend who had recently been released from prison. I drove from Denver and operated amateur radio in the car part of the way. Tijuana itself was a driving challenge with the traffic circles and navigating entering and exiting Mexico. On two Sundays I wanted to visit "El Faro: The Border Church," a gathering that includes a Sunday service held simultaneously on both sides of the tall border fence in what is called "Friendship Park," with communion being served on both sides (you can just make out the raised cup on the US side through the mesh). I tried to visit it twice, once on the US side and once on the Mexican side. The US side was accessible only by a hike around a flooded road, rough land, and beach. It was clear my scooter would never make the journey. So, my successful visit was on the Mexican side. I watched families try to touch each other through the mesh fence and share in moments of contact. This ministry has been going for a long

time, and provides some comfort and witness to our common humanity. *Sojourners* magazine describes the church meeting ...at Friendship Park, or "El Parque de la Amistad," the piece of land that lies between the mesh border fence and the larger border wall that keeps the United States separate from Mexico. Usually, the outer wall is closed, cordoning off any opportunities for people on opposite sides of the border to connect. But for four hours each weekend it opens. For most people, the border is a place of division. But for Pastor John Fanestil, the borderland, or "la fronteriza," is "a place of encounter." (sojo.net/magazine/january-2019/inside-america-s-border-church, retrieved 6/15/23)

My friend was not a church-goer, so he didn't attend with me. But I had hoped my time with this newly-released inmate would be helpful. Ultimately, however, the trip ended the friendship, since my friend proved he couldn't be trusted because of the lies and misrepresentations he made to me. It was my last attempt to help an inmate.

Other travels have included flying to several Western Methodist Justice Movement (WMJM) gatherings on the West Coast. A gathering in 2008 in San Diego, prior to a meeting of the Western Jurisdiction Leadership Team, was sponsored by the California-Pacific chapter of the Methodist Federation for Social Action. This gathering planted the seeds for the formation of WMJM in 2012. The first large gathering of WMJM was in Lake Tahoe, to which we drove with Bryan, a friend from the Open Door Church and an amateur radio operator. It was a really good trip, through Yellowstone Park, parts of Idaho, Utah, and Nevada. The gathering was a formative moment for the movement and included justice activists from all over the Western

Jurisdiction. One of the speakers was from Canada and was a minister whose home church was in Africa. His perspective helped broaden our understanding greatly. Another gathering

was in Portland, where racial justice was a focus.

When Maggie worked at the Hospice of Metro Denver (now The Denver Hospice), she traveled to Tanzania to volunteer as a chaplain for the hospice in Arusha. On her way home, she and I met in Frankfurt, Germany, and traveled by train to Amsterdam. She was so tired that I explored the city one day on my own on my three-wheel scooter. I was disappointed to learn when I tried to ride the street-car train system that I was not allowed, even though the platform was clearly marked with the universal disability access symbol. Not knowing Dutch and not having any knowledge about the local customs and rules, I accepted that and just scooted where I needed to go. On my way to one place, I happened to pass through the red-light district, and exchanged smiles and silent greetings with the women sitting in the picture windows. I didn't even think about going in, so I don't know if their establishments would've been accessible! Maggie got to go into Anne Frank's house but it wasn't accessible to me. I was entranced by the cathedrals, particularly the one in Köln (Cologne). I had boned up on the German I learned a bit in college, but realized I didn't know it well enough to be useful: one clerk suggested, "Just use English."

Our travels have taken us to nine countries, and all US states except six. One country not mentioned above was Maggie's overnight stay in South Africa when her flight for the last leg to Tanzania was canceled. Her hospice companions who had traveled separately were worried, but her assertiveness and cab drivers helped her have an uneventful stay. Another time, she traveled to Fiji with folks from Open Door Community Church to paint and maintain a small chapel there. Her passport slipped out of her purse on the plane to Los Angeles, which necessitated an overnight stay in LA and an emergency replacement—the original was sent to her several months later by the airline.

Another memorable trip was to England on a tour of John Wesley-related sites, including his birth home and Wesley's Chapel in London. We were part of a tour group in a large coach, and I was using a three-wheel scooter. The scooter traveled in the luggage compartment under the bus, and was loaded and unloaded by several attendees. The only inaccessible place that I remember was Wesley's birth home in Epworth. I enjoyed imagining Wesley preaching at Wesley's Chapel. I enjoyed the scenic tour around England, which included Bath, Cotswalds, and Epworth.

As I've described before, we've been to a number of the national parks. We took a tour with another couple of Canyonlands. It was in a four-wheel-drive vehicle and at one place we drove through we were within four inches on each side of the vehicle! At another, a turn took a back-up maneuver. The scenery was awesome. The "road" in several places was just relatively flat rock—and not smooth, either! We ate lunch at this spot, showing the beauty of the place.

Maggie's chaplaincy gave her the opportunity in the  2000s to participate in several annual national gatherings of chaplains sponsored by the United Methodist Endorsing Agency, usually on the West Coast, either at a Catholic retreat center or Asilomar. I was able to attend the lectures that were of interest to me as a former pastoral counselor. One exercise that was particularly powerful was one where we were to pair up with one other person and look into each other's eyes for five or 10 minutes (whatever time it was, it was an eternity). It was powerful to meet another person in this totally nonverbal way. The connection was truly an I-Thou (Martin Buber's term) experience.

Another memorable trip was to Alliance, Nebraska, to see the solar eclipse of August 21, 2017. We took a less-traveled route, starting before sunup that morning, and went through significant fog. We parked in the parking lot across from Alliance First United Methodist Church. The eclipse was as incredible as everyone who sees one first-hand says. We drove out to see Carhenge afterwards but then missed being in the initial line of cars leaving Alliance. We drove in a solid line of cars for miles. It took us over six hours to get home!

FOURTEEN

Concluding Thoughts

So, there you have it. The arc of my life, deep details here, public appearances there, loves, joys, enjoyable and not-so-enjoyable times, an attempt at a "coherent narrative."

What have I learned over the past over 77 years? Obviously, I've learned a lot, some very technical, some very mundane, some deeply personal, and some very relevant to human relationships.

I've learned to seek to be as present with my internal "sea" of consciousness as I'm able. This is an on-going growth area. Part of this is to develop and nurture a compassionate "friendship" with all parts of my internal reality: the memories, the sensations, the awarenesses, the intuitions, the urgings of various parts of my brain (as Siegel has been teaching), and the hopes, dreams, plans, and celebrations of my life.

I've learned to commit to and work towards clarity of my communications not only internally but especially with those I love. I've learned to do my best to reframe less productive thoughts into more productive and healthy ones.

I've learned a lot about sexuality. Did I "figure it out"? I think I've figured it out, at least for me, and Jim Nelson's succinct definition sums it up: "Sexuality is a sign, a symbol, and a means of our call to communication and communion." In other words, we are created for community, to be in communion with our Creator and with other human beings, and sexuality is a sign, a symbol, and a means of our celebration of this communication, community, and communion with each other. We were created different from each other, a differentiation witnessed in the creation story in the Bible, but with gender and sexuality differences that we now know are non-binary continua in all respects, with all kinds of gradations and complications. I believe that communion can happen in mutual pleasuring and happens best in deep and lasting relationships, where the depth and best of each person can be experienced and celebrated over time and shared experiences. I also think that meaningful sexual expression can happen in less "deep and lasting" relationships, but nonetheless, where the "best of each person" can still be experienced (albeit perhaps less fully) and celebrated in shorter relationships. I think there is a deep human (maybe even soul?) meeting that is almost built into the sexual exchange that calls us into more than "just" mutual pleasuring. The key is the relationship and its qualities.

In light of these conclusions about sexuality, I think one must ask about the quality of the relationship that might have existed between me and the anonymous person in the hospital episode described earlier. It is impossible to be sure since the memory is so fragmentary, but while there were some pleasurable aspects for me and presumably for that person, the relationship would hardly have been very equal: an adult, undoubtedly a caregiver of some kind, and a child under their care in a hospital. The difference in age and experience in addition to the issues around consent and the restrictive command accompanying the experience made it on balance harmful as described.

Did I figure myself out? I think I've come close, and I recognize

I'm still "in process," still growing, still learning. You can see the issues of attachment, abandonment, early sexual experience, abuse, and my attempts to heal in the story of my life, not just to "figure it out for myself," but with the help of many people, including therapists, along the way, and to use what I have learned to help others who want it. The impact of the personal disaster of polio for a two-year-old and its early treatment and my response to it at the time set me up for a lifetime of wondering, searching, questioning, and finally grieving and accepting the realities of my life. The flawed attachment I developed set up the questions of identity and strength of self outlined in the Preface. It's unclear to me how far I've been able to transcend much beyond *The Farther Reaches of Human Nature* (Maslow, 1971). I think I've been able to transcend and continue to grow from most of the trauma and loss of my early years. I hope I've been helpful to others along the way.

And where did I get the strength to be able to feel like I needed to "figure it out for myself" and have the hope to get me through the abandonment/detachment? Remember the quote about hope above, "Hope is the belief that your future can be brighter and better than your past and that you actually have a role to play in making it better." I recently found myself singing (in my head only!) in the shower "Oh God Our Help in Ages Past" ("our hope for years to come…"). It occurred to me that by the time I came down with polio at age two years five months, I had already heard as a very young child my dad preach and lead worship for two years, and probably heard that hymn at least a couple of times. The words themselves I would likely not have understood, but the emotional tone underneath them would have come through. The depth and hope of his version of Christianity probably gave me the hope that I could make it through and find a brighter future—though I would have no idea what that might be like for many years to come.

How was I able to accomplish as much as I have through

the various jobs, roles, and positions I've held? I've been blessed with a good and curious mind that has provided me with the capability to learn as well as to make (sometimes unusual) connections between concepts and experiences. Many people over the years have provided constructive feedback on my efforts, most of it affirming my skills, capabilities, and accomplishments. I once described to Maggie that I sometimes felt like I had a good platform but it rested on shaky ground: all the intellectual learning has been good but the unresolved early experiences didn't give me a solid emotional foundation. At times, I have doubted myself and seemed to lack the emotional strength to handle the inevitable challenges that come to everyone who strives to achieve.

But to summarize what I've come to in my quest for identity and self-understanding: I am a person who has a curiosity about many things, how things work, what are the connections between things and ideas, whether they be issues of faith, music, the universe, electronics, or computer programs and operating systems. I've enjoyed the many experiences I've had in the varied fields.

I've had some wonderful times, some interesting times, some incredible joy (almost always surrounding music), and many tears in uncovering the origin of the sadness that has dogged me most of my life. I believe that the depth of the experiences I've described, even when not fully conscious, led to whatever empathy and gentleness that I've been able to offer and respond to.

One of the biggest mistakes I made led to much regret. The boundary violation that caused my loss of AAPC membership also ended my career as a minister in the UMC. I've discovered and understood why it happened and realize that I had insufficient awareness of the dynamics that led to it. And I have struggled to forgive myself for this and other mistakes, and I hope that those I have hurt will find it in their hearts to forgive me (and perhaps themselves for any part they might have had).

My friends have recently observed that my ministry has actually continued, though not in a formal, traditional way. It has continued primarily through the caucuses and ministries of my church, on the local, regional and wider levels, working for increased understanding of sexuality and faith, and for justice, acceptance and inclusion of LGBTQIA+ persons in The United Methodist Church. And I've also continued to try as best as I might to treat people with openness, respect, and helpfulness, not just in the church but outside, using as much of myself and my skills and knowledge as is appropriate.

So, I understand that life is a journey of discovery, experimentation, success, failure, growth, and deepening faith in the holiness of living and sharing. I hope that something that I've written has helped you in your own journey of life. You are a blessed child of the universe!

PART III
ADDENDA

Image/Captions for *A Boy Survives*

Front Cover	Benny (young Ben) in a swing in Arkansas
Front Cover	The Milky Way, taken in Maui by William Zhang
Page 6	Parents, Joe and Enid, early in their marriage
Page 6	Dad, Joe, in his early 20s
Page 7	Dad, Rev. Joe Roe, a Nebraska Methodist minister in his 40s
Page 8	Mom, Enid, in her diaconal minister robe, age 60
Page 9	Mom, Enid as a young adult
Page 9	Mom, Enid in her later years
Page 10	Sister, Phyllis Roe, as a seminary student at Union Seminary in New York
Page 11	Sister Phyllis at her desk at the Samaritan Counseling Center Hawai'i
Page 12	Sister, Rebecca, known to her friends as Becky, at 26
Page 12	The banner Rebecca made as she learned to live with SLE
Page 13	Sister, Deb, at her desk at Leclede Groves Chaplains Office
Page 14	Benny (Ben), age four weeks
Page 15	Benny (Ben), walking, on first birthday
Page 16	Benny (Ben) in a swing at about five, in Arkansas at grandmother's house
Page 19	Sister Phyllis and Benny on the steps to Dad's office in the church at Bayard
Page 21	How Benny learned to write with his left hand
Page 21	How a friend writes with his left hand
Page 24	The four Roe kids on wheels
Page 27	1970 all-solid-state communications receiver from R.L. Drake
Page 28	Ben in eighth grade band uniform holding French horn

Page 29	Letter patch for going to the Orange Bowl with the Ainsworth band
Page 32	Ben as high school senior
Page 36	Ben's first ham station, in the Ainsworth parsonage basement
Page 36	Ben's second ham station, in his Ainsworth parsonage bedroom
Page 40	The Dock Brief sign of play where Ben met Maggie
Page 47	A banner Ben helped paint in about 1972 that hung on the chapel at Claremont School of Theology
Page 51	The large two-inch Ampex quadruplex videotape recorder used for playback of premium movies at Theta Cable Television in 1975
Page 55	The old milk can with a bouquet for an Easter sermon at Endicott UMC
Page 66	Our Victorian Baker neighborhood house in Denver on Delaware Street
Page 67	Warren Methodist Church sanctuary in 1910
Page 69	Warren United Methodist Church Christmas Eve 2013
Page 73	Ben onsite at one of the power plants in the U.S. Virgin Islands
Page 74	Benny, 1953, about age seven
Page 75	The office of the Rocky Mountain Conference in about 2009
Page 79	Arvada UMC sign and parking lot, showing the sanctuary building
Page 80	Home in Arvada, after xeriscaping the front yard
Page 81	One of the three paintings by Maggie's dad, Rev. Larry Davis in 1974 (Wave)
Page 82	Two more paintings by Maggie's dad, Rev. Larry Davis (Forest Stream and Glacier Lake)

Page 86	Benny contemplating life in his sandbox in Strong, Arkansas
Page 87	The Tammen building of Denver's Children's Hospital in about 1958
Page 92	Benny, a week before coming down with polio, September 1948
Page 118	Blair Blurbs: the masthead of the first issue of the newsletter of Affirmation at GC, 1976
Page 119	An image of the MHS letterhead
Page 130	A patron reads the Affirmation page of the broadsheet newspaper of LYNC
Page 135	Maggie at the tree behind the old library at NWU, probably about 1966
Page 136	Maggie and Ben exiting the church after our wedding in 1969
Page 137	A portrait of our dog Sandy taken about 1979
Page 137	Ben and Maggie's 10th anniversary celebration
Page 139	Rings, made for their tenth anniversary
Page 141	Maggie's graduation from Iliff School of Theology in 1999
Page 141	Ben and Maggie's 53rd anniversary at the Denver Cheesecake Factory
Page 147	Ben playing a double horn in scooter at AUMC with a horn holder he made
Page 153	The fortieth anniversary celebration of the RCP/RMN in Charlotte, NC
Page 153	The White House across Lafayette Park in Washington DC in October, 2023
Page 154	Ben and Maggie on their way home from their COVID-blessed stay in a DC
Page 154	Communion service at the El Faro Friendship Park at the Tijuana Border

Page 155	The communion table at the El Faro Friendship Park at the Tijuana Border
Page 155	A scene from the first WMJM retreat at Lake Tahoe in 2014
Page 156	Ben and Maggie in western Wyoming on the way to Tahoe with friend Bryan
Page 156	Maggie blessing a group of boys in Arusha, Tanzania, near the hospice
Page 157	Maggie and Ben had lunch in this gorgeous spot in Canyonlands National Park
Page 158	At one of Maggie's retreats with the United Methodist Endorsing Agency at Asilomar in California
Page 158	Photo of the 2017 solar eclipse taken in Oregon by my friend Greg Nelson

Photo credits/Permissions

My friends Bryan Burrma and Greg Nelson have given formal permission to use their photos on pages 156 and 158 respectively.. The large photo of the Milky Way photo of the Milky Way was taken on Maui by William Zhang, (unsplash.com/photos/blue-and-white-starry-night-sky-hqKPgEVEc-8).

All the others were taken by me or by family members. A few are by unknown persons.

Annotated Bibliography

Some of the books and articles that have been important or helpful in my journey, as well as some other resources that may be of interest:

Linda Alsop-Shields and Heather Mohay, "John Bowlby and James Robertson: theorists, scientists and crusaders for improvements in the care of children in hospital," *Journal of Advanced Nursing,* 2001 Jul v35(1):50-8. (Helpful outlining the importance of how consequential for children the polices of care in the hospital are.)

Derrick Sherwin Bailey, *Sexual Relation in Christian Thought.* NY: Harper, 1959. (A groundbreaking book.)

Richard Bolles, *What Color Is Your Parachute?* Berkeley: Ten Speed Press, 1978. (A key to my discovering my first career path.)

Dietrich Bonhoeffer, *Letters and Papers from Prison,* NY: Macmillan, 1953, paperback ed. 1962. (A classic.)

Marcus J. Borg, *The Heart of Christianity: Rediscovering A Life Of Faith.* San Francisco: HarperCollins, 2003. (A progressive approach to Christianity.)

Marcus J. Borg, *Reading the Bible Again For the First Time: Taking the Bible Seriously But Not Literally.* San Francisco: HarperSanFrancisco, 2001 (An important way of approaching the text of the Bible.)

John Boswell, *Christianity, Social Tolerance, and Homosexuality: Gay People in Western Europe from the Beginning of the Christian Era to the Fourteenth Century.* Chicago: University of Chicago Press, 1980. (A groundbreaking study showing that gay people were not always treated badly.)

The Boy Mechanic. A Popular Mechanics Book, NY: Simon and Schuster, 1955. (Lots of projects for a young person.)

Alla Renée Bozarth, *Life is Goodbye, Life is Hello.* Compcare Publications, 1985. (A classic about the grief process.)

Karl Heinz Brisch, *Treating Attachment Disorders; From Theory to Therapy,* Second Edition. NY, London: Guilford Press, 2014. (A good outline of the theory and some possibilities for treatment.)

Frederick Buechner, *Wishful Thinking; A Seeker's ABC,* Revised and expanded. NY: HarperOne, 1993. (One of the sources for the quote on vocation.)

Howard J. and Charlotte H. Clinebell, *The Intimate Marriage.* NY: Harper & Row, 1970. (Important for us in the early years of our marriage, encouraging us to see intimacy as encompassing much more than just sex!)

John B. Cobb and David Ray Griffith, *Process Theology: An Introductory Exposition.* Louisville: Westminster John Knox Press, 1976. (A helpful introduction to Process Theology.)

Larry L. and Joan M. Constantine, *Group Marriage: A Study of Contemporary Multilateral Marriage.* NY: Collier, 1973. (Very helpful chapter on jealousy.)

Larry L. Constantine, Floyd M. Martinson, Editors, *Children and Sex: New Findings, New Perspectives,* Boston: Little, Brown, 1981 (A rare look at childhood sexuality.)

Evelyn Millis Duval, *Facts of Life and Love for Teenagers.* NY: Popular Library, 1957 [1950] (My first book on sex!)

John E. Fortunato, *Embracing the Exile: Healing Journeys of Gay Christians.* NY: Seabury, 1982. (A source of hope and of a much deeper way of dealing with being LGBTQIA+, especially for COG.)

Christine E. Gudorf, *Body, Sex, and Pleasure: Reconstructing Christian Sexual Ethics.* Cleveland, Pilgrim Press, 1994. (Knowledgeable about the science of sexual differentiation and how an ethic based on the binary is unhelpful.)

Casey Gwinn and Chan Hellman, *Hope Rising: How the Science of HOPE Can Change Your Life.* NY: Morgan James, 2018. (Helpful definition of hope, and living with hope.)

Carolyn G. Heilbrun, *Toward a Recognition of Androgyny.* NY: W. W. Norton, 1982. (Androgyny could help us better understood gender role expectations and even what gender is.)

Loraine Hutchins and Lani Kaahumanu, eds., *Bi Any Other Name: Bisexual People Speak Out.* Boston: Alyson Publications, 1991. (A good source of stories and experiences of folks who identify as bisexual.)

Robert Karen, *Becoming Attached; First Relationships and How They Shape Our Capacity to Love.* New York: Oxford University Press, 1998. (A masterful explanation and history of attachment theory.)

Miriam Kaufman, Cory Silverberg, and Fran Odette, *The Ultimate Guide to Sex and Disability; For All of Us Who Live With Disabilities, Chronic Pain, and Illness.* San Francisco: Clais, 2007. (Canadian writers provide an enlightening sex-positive and disability-positive guide to exploring one's own sexuality, affirming the many ways bodies and ways of being sexual differ.)

Fritz Klein and Timothy J. Wolf, eds., *Two Lives to Lead: Bisexuality in Men and Women.* NY: Harrington Park Press, 1985. (Gave us some clues in dealing with my "bisexuality".)

Barry Kohn and Alice Matusow, *Barry and Alice: Portrait of a Bisexual Marriage.* Englewood Cliffs, N.J.: Prentice-Hall, 1980. (A bisexual couple share how they work with their bisexuality.)

John Lewellen, *The Boy Scientist.* A Popular Mechanics Book, NY: Simon and Schuster, 1955. (A good introduction to the sciences for a ten-year-old.)

Abraham Maslow, *The Farther Reaches of Human Nature.* Arkana/Penguin Books, 1971. (An introduction to humanistic and transpersonal psychology.)

James F. Masterson, *The Search for the Real Self: Unmasking the Personality Disorders of Our Age.* NY: Free Press, 1988. (Helped me better understand some of my clients and gave me clues on healthy development.)

James F. Masterson, *The Real Self: A Developmental, Self, and Object Relations Approach: Structure, Function, Development, Psychopathology, Treatment, Creativity.* NY: Brunner/Mazel, 1985. (Helpful in understanding the task of individuation and and separation of the young child.)

John J. McNeil, *The Church and the Homosexual.* Kansas City: Sheed Andrews and McMeel, 1976. (A classic exploration of the irony of the way the church treats gay people based on a false reading of the story of Sodom.)

Alice Miller, *The Drama of the Gifted Child: The Search for the True Self.* NY: Basic Books, 1981. (This book helped me acknowledge my emotional truth.)

Alice Miller, *Thou Shalt Not Be Aware: Society's Betrayal of the Child.* Farrar, Straus and Giroux, 1984. (How society's silence on child sexual abuse harms childhood development.)

Alice Miller, *For Your Own Good: Hidden Cruelty in Child-rearing and the Roots of Violence.* Farrar, Straus and Giroux, 1983. (How some child-rearing is cruel and leads to adult violence.)

James B. Nelson, *Embodiment: An Approach to Sexuality and Christian Theology.* Minneapolis: Augsburg, 1979. (A ground-breaking, sex-positive and realistic approach to human sexuality and Christian theology.)

Reinhold Niebuhr, *The Nature and Destiny of Man: A Christian Interpretation: Volume One: Human Nature; Volume Two: Human Destiny.* NY: Charles Scribner's Sons, 1941. (A classic in the theology of human nature.)

Thomas O'Carroll, "Childhood 'Innocence' is Not Ideal: Virtue Ethics and Child–Adult Sex," published by Springer, retrieved 5/26/2023 (an argument for a different way of looking at the purpose of sex.)

Karen P. Oliveto, *Our Strangely Warmed Hearts: Coming Out Into God's Call,* Nashville: Abingdon, 2018. (A thorough look at Christian LGBTQ people and the United Methodist struggles with sexuality, 1972-2018.)

Charles M. Olsen, *The Base Church: Creating Community Through Multiple Forms.* Atlanta: Forum House, 1973. (The source of some of the rationale behind Community of Grace in Lincoln.)

Nena and George O'Neill, *Open Marriage: A New Life Style for Couples,* New York: Evans, 1972. (Helpful for communication, flexible roles, equality, and jealousy issues.)

Linda T. Sanford, *Strong At The Broken Places: Overcoming the Trauma of Childhood Abuse.* NY: Random House, 1990. (A hopeful book giving guidance in overcoming trauma.)

Sela, Maya, "The Trauma of a Gifted Child Whose Mother Was Alice Miller," Haaretzcom, July 12, 2014.

Daniel Siegel, *Mindsight: The New Science of Personal Transformation,* NY: Bantam, 2010. (This was the breakthrough book for me in putting words to my emotional experience with polio.)

Daniel Siegel, *The Power of Showing Up: How Parental Presence Shapes Who Our Kids Become and How Their Brains Get Wired.* NY: Ballantine, 2020. (Important book on parenting and attachment.)

James R. Smith and Lynn G. Smith, eds., *Beyond Monogamy: Recent Studies of Sexual Alternatives in Marriage.* Baltimore: John Hopkins University Press, 1974. (Helpful research into marriage in the early seventies.)

Leslie Weatherhead, *The Will of God.* Nashville: Abingdon, 1999 [1944]. (Helpful to this questioning teen.)

Leslie Weatherhead, *The Christian Agnostic.* Nashville: Abingdon, 1965. (Helpful to this questioning teen.)

Ken Wilber, *The Atman Project: A Transpersonal View of Human Development.* Wheaton, IL: Quest Books, 1980. (One main point of this book is that in each stage, the person assumes they've reached their highest level and have resistance to progressing higher.)

Ken Wilber, Jack Engler, and Daniel P. Brown, *Transformations of Consciousness: Conventional and Contemplative Perspectives on Development.* Boston: Shambhala New Science Library, 1986. (The chapter on developmental "lesions" was most helpful.)

Links:

There are lots of helpful articles available these days on the World Wide Web. Here are a few I've found in addition to ones linked in the text above.

My biography in the LGBTQ Religious Archives, 2021. There are many more biographies here. lgbtqreligiousarchives.org/profiles/ben-roe

On healing from attachment and abandonment issues: www.psychologytoday.com/us/blog/compassion-matters/201802/healing-attachment-issues (Refers to Siegel's *Mindsight* insights.)

integrativepsych.co/new-blog/heal-your-anxiety-long-island (As I read this, I realized I'd done all 10 steps they outline.)

On the origin of the "incompatibility" clause in the UMC Book of Discipline: archives.gcah.org/handle/10516/9938

More on the early history of the UMC and the gay liberation movement: lgbtqreligiousarchives.org/profiles/ted-mcilvenna and exhibits.lgbtran.org/exhibits/show/crh/

Some Polio Resources

Richard L Bruno, *The Polio Paradox: Uncovering the Hidden History of Polio To Understand and Treat "Post-Polio Syndrome" and Chronic Fatigue.* New York: Warner Books, 2002. (A wide-ranging book to understand polio and its late effects, including ways to manage life with PPS.)

Lauro S. Halstead, *Managing Post-Polio: A Guide to Living and Aging Well with Post-Polio Syndrome.* Washington, D.C.: NRH Press, 2nd ed., 2006. (A classic guide for understanding and managing PPS.)

Julie K. Silver, *Post-Polio: A Guide for Polio Surivors and their Families.* New Haven: Yale University Press, 2001.

Links:

post-polio.org The Post-Polio Health International collects, preserves and makes available research and knowledge to promote the well-being and independence of polio survivors, home ventilator users, their caregivers and families, and to support the health professionals who treat them.

polioplace.org "This website, Polio Place, is written mostly in English, but can be automatically translated by Google Translate."

www.who.int/health-topics/poliomyelitis World Health Organization on Polio

www.postpolioinfo.com/centre.php The International Center for Polio Education (Richard Bruno)

Polio Survivor's Handbook (www.postpolioinfo.com/handbook.php), a downloadable eBook with a protocol that has been found to successfully treat Post-Polio Sequelae.

www.who.int/health-topics/poliomyelitis World Health Organization on Polio

Appendix A: Meditation on Disability and Body Image

Our bodies are our connection to our world: we experience the world through them and the world experiences us through them. Our bodies are unique; even "identical" twins from the same fertilized egg have differences, though often not obvious.

Our bodies are shaped by many factors, from DNA from the individuals whose DNA we carry, to hormones, prenatal conditions, to the myriad experiences after birth. Some of these differences limit or challenge one's experience of the world (spina bifida, lack of sight or hearing, for example). Disease, accidents, and violence can also change one's body shape or features.

My explanation as a toddler for how I got polio was, "I ate dirt." That experience of polio at age 2 ½ years was life-changing. It shaped, and in some ways limited how I experienced the world. For some people, it limited their experience of me. For instance, I was always the last chosen for kickball in grade school because my running was slower and more awkward than the others.

Being in two hospitals for three months with only hour-long visits from parents once a week was one of the worst parts of the experience.

Having a weak right hip and leg affected the way I walked and made me stand out. In college my nickname was "bouncy." This feature caught the eye of a young woman who became my life-long friend, partner, companion, and lover for over 50 years. My disability was intriguing to her. Her interest and caring has been a critical source of support as I've dealt with the aftereffects of polio and the onset of the "late effects" of polio years later.

Interests and hobbies in childhood changed the focus from disability to ability and capability.

Discovering and eventually affirming my attractions to other males was a challenge we both took on to explore and integrate. This led to our involvement with the LGBTQ community and organizations like Affirmation, RCP and RMN in the United

Methodist Church, and PFLAG.

As I have continued to learn about human sexuality and gender, I realized that the term "bisexual" was too binary for me, as, in fact, I found myself attracted to some individuals without even knowing their gender identity.

If our bodies are our connection to the world, how our bodies are perceived by others is important. In many societies, there are rough standards about "attractiveness," "beauty," and "desirability." For folks with visible disabilities or shapes and features which don't fit these "standards," finding acceptance, friendship and love can be a big challenge.

Finding places to meet others like oneself is important. However, if a gathering place is not accessible to those in mobility devices like wheelchairs, scooters or walkers, it means this physical means of connecting with others like oneself becomes another isolating experience.

Now, when we get right down to seeing another in a swim suit or without, there is always the common anxiety: How will I be perceived? Will I be affirmed by this other? Will my body be "acceptable"? And if there is a spark of sexual interest, will it still be there after the other sees my body?

Of course body image is not only an issue for LGBTQIA+ individuals: I suspect we all could use exercises which enhance our own body image, to be able to look at ourselves through the loving eyes of the Creator who made each of us, who created us, and is still creating us.

Our bodies can be the embodiment of love, through which we can express and receive caring, attentiveness, and loving.

Ultimately and ideally, we can transcend the forms, the shapes, and the limits of our physical bodies and truly meet each other as the spiritual, embodied human beings we are, who can embody holy love with each other.

— Presented to Post-Polio Group by Ben Roe, 2021

Appendix B: Coming Out As a Bi Believer

A National Coming Out Day Speech, 2004
Mountain View Community Church, Aurora, CO

I once presented a workshop on heterosexism to the adult church school class at Warren United Methodist, where I am a member. At one point, someone asked me what my personal interest was in the subject. I answered simply, "I have been aware of and have affirmed my same-gender attractions for a long time." It had taken me a long time to be able to say this.

My partner Maggie and I have been married over 35 years now, but in our 8th year, I found myself very unsettled as I read Don Clark's *Loving Someone Gay*. I was unsettled because I recognized myself in his (broad) definition of "Being Gay." I realized at that moment the significance of some feelings I had had for a seminary classmate.

That was the start of my coming out journey. It took me a bit longer to understand myself as "bisexual."

Maggie and I did some very helpful therapy in those early years around communication, intimacy, commitment, fidelity, and how to integrate my bisexuality into our marriage as we built a new understanding of ourselves and our relationship.

We became active in the gay and lesbian communities as one way to express our new relationship. We helped start a welcoming house church, a PFLAG chapter, and participated in political support for Lesbian and Gay civil rights, because we felt this would help make the world a better place for lesbians and gay men, as well as bisexual folks. Maggie often tells how being introduced to the gay community has helped her own coming out as a powerful advocate for the marginalized and how she has found a community of wonderful friends.

My coming out bi was made more difficult at first because I was stuck in the common either-or dichotomy of gay/straight. The Kinsey scale was a great revelation to me because it helped me begin to move away from dichotomous thinking to continuum-thinking. The Klein Grid and its derivatives from Keppel and Hamilton were even more helpful.

My coming out bi was more difficult because most churches have actively fought against a more full understanding of sexuality and because the gay and lesbian communities also have been slow to come to a fuller understanding of sexuality.

Faith has always been an important part of my life, so I found the gay United Methodist caucus and attended my first meeting soon after I first self-identified as bi. I identified as bi at one point and was told that bisexuality was not their agenda. But because we were committed to an agenda larger than ourselves and working towards greater inclusiveness and openness to the diversity of sexuality within our church, we worked locally and didn't put much energy into that group for several years. Fourteen years later, I helped lead a workshop on bisexuality for them and the outcome was much better.

My coming out bi was helped by The Experience, a workshop that grew out of the gay community and helps participants live with increased personal power, integrity and love. Working as an ally in the gay and lesbian and now Gay, Lesbian, Bi, and Transgender movement is a simple matter of justice and a matter of working toward a more healthy understanding of sexuality.

My coming out bi was helped by the church as well, because I had heard the word of inclusion and grace all my life and because the church provided the sexuality education experiences which included principles that allowed me to grow into a new self-understanding.

I've chosen to work for inclusiveness within the church because I identify also as a follower of Jesus and because the church has been such a negative and persecuting force regarding sexuality.

Acknowledging my bisexuality has allowed me to become more free to celebrate the gifts I have received from life. My experience of being bi has been in some ways another experience of "exile" like my experiences of polio as a young child, of sexual abuse, and of growing up as a preacher's kid. John Fortunato's book *Embracing the Exile: Healing Journeys of Gay Christians* spoke deeply to me. Being in exile has given me, like it did John Fortunato and the Hebrew people, a deeper faith. It has also given me a deeper sense of compassion for others.

Being bi has also given me perhaps a more direct appreciation of the truth of James B. Nelson's definition of sexuality in his book Embodiment: sexuality is a sign, a symbol, and a means of our call to communication and communion. My ability to fully love individuals regardless of gender and to transcend gender roles usually has been a delightful source of personal and spiritual enrichment. My ability to see a range of options in many areas and my ability to think more in continua than in dichotomies has been another gift of being bi.

Perhaps discussion of bisexuality will help move us into a more accurate and deeper understanding of sexuality. The easy and false dichotomies of heterosexual-homosexual, male-female, and masculine-feminine will give way to models and paradigms of human sexuality that better match the realities of healthy, real-life sexuality. Perhaps we can move some day to "just sexuality," without worrying about the gender of the person to whom our affections and attractions are directed. Just as I hope we will come some day to a place where we emphasize ability and capability rather than disability.

I have found that when people deal openly with their sexuality, they become more free, more tolerant, and more fully human. I celebrate this time where all can deal more openly with sexuality and move towards greater freedom, acceptance, and wholeness.

Since this speech, I've continued to develop my thought about what sexuality and sexual orientation and gender identity mean. One very important learning experience I attended was the Earl Lectures of Pacific School of Religion in 2005, entitled "Sex and the City of God." One lecture in particular gave me a big boost in understanding. It was by Christine Gudorf, "Is An Ethic of Sex Even Possible," based on her work acknowledging the more recent scientific understandings of human sexuality, of the at least six variables which form human sexuality (hormones, genetics, internal and external features, etc.) and in which each is a continuum, not a binary. And so as I've met more folks who are either trans or non-binary, and as I've recognized attractions to some of them, I've realized that I need to change the description of my orientation this way: "I recognize and celebrate my attractions to individuals of any gender."

—Ben Roe, 2004

Appendix C: What Do We Know About Sexuality?

(Written for the Love Your Neighbor Coalition Newsletter at the 2016 General Conference of The United Methodist Church)

When I was in high school, I talked my dad into letting our youth group leaders present the Methodist "Sex and the Whole Person" course. It was helpful, but I still wondered what the big deal was with sex and sexuality. Why did it cause such giggles, whispers, and fear?

When I was in college, I figured out more, but on my own time after classes and in Methodist Student Movement. Still questions. Why the silence? Why the hushed tones? Why the whispered gossip?

When I was in seminary, things began to get a bit clearer, thanks to a couple of classes and team-written papers. I got exposed to a wide range of people and sexuality ideas. A major paper helped me work out some of it using the thought of a major theologian and comparing and contrasting two church sex education programs for youth.

But in my first parish, things got more confusing, as I met the conflict between sex as reproduction only, and sexuality as a whole system of values, beliefs, and practices. And I met a man who wanted help with his homosexuality. More whispers, more fear, more hushed talk.

As I got to know first gay men, then lesbian women, then bisexual people, my horizons expanded. I learned about the continuum of sexual orientation: when persons are attracted to others and which sexes catch their eye.

I had noticed the inequality between men and women from my growing up in a family with 3 sisters. I had become a feminist man, and noticed the ways sexism imprisons men as well as women. I found the wonderful recording, "Free To Be You and Me." I learned about the continuum between "masculine" and "feminine."

As I have been involved more and more in the movements of Affirmation: United Methodists for LGBTQI Concerns and the

Reconciling Ministries Network, I have noticed more things about sexuality: how integral it seems to be in our individual and cultural searches for identity and community, and how social and legal inequality impacts real human beings who might be different from the norm.

But most importantly, I have learned about the six biological markers of human sexuality, and how each one is a continuum! Talk about complexity! There is a continuum of chromosomal sex, of external genital structures, of internal sexual organs, of gonadal tissue, and even of brain structure! I learned about, but even more importantly, met real human beings whose experience of gender and sexuality didn't fit the binary categories of "male" or "female" and all the cultural constructions which are built up around these two concepts.

And these persons were Christian believers, who shared a faith journey much like mine, with questions, discoveries, and ultimately commitments of faith that felt a lot like mine.

Along with all these discoveries about sexuality, I was discovering how large God is, that God could actually create a complexity like this, and call it good--even delight in it! That God could delight in the meaning that God's human creatures were creating out of it, and delight in the relationship that God could have with each one in a Divine relationship!

Part of this discovery was that Jesus seemed quite OK with the diversity around him of human beings who were trying their best to make a success out of their lives, even when they were racked by "leprosy," disabilities, and social exclusion. He reached out to each one and challenged them to go deeper in their relationship with God.

So why can't our United Methodist Church embrace the complexity that God has created and is creating in human sexuality, and reach out like Jesus did to welcome, celebrate, and invite into a deeper relationship with the Divine?

Ben Roe is a former pastor, pastoral counselor and sexuality educator. In retirement, he devotes his time to advocacy with Affirmation, RMN, and the Western Methodist Justice Movement.

Appendix D: A Word About My Faith Commitments
(from JBenjaminRoe.com)

The upheaval in The United Methodist Church over the passage (in 2019) of a legalistic, punitive, and graceless set of new "laws" in the United Methodist rulebook, the Book of Discipline, has helped me clarify my own commitments of faith. Yes, I'm former clergy (Nebraska Conference) but never have I been so clear as I am right now that these are the central commitments and values in my faith journey:

I'm committed to inclusion and to Wesley's emphasis on grace. God's grace is for all, preveniently (before someone even knows God), justifying (as one comes into communion with God), and sancifying (as one grows in grace).

Living in grace includes living with respect for all people, beings, and creation, even when these might threaten to overwhelm, harm, and just plain disagree.

Sin is "missing the mark" of the good life God has for each person uniquely, based on our gifts and graces as given by God in the first place.

Forgiveness is offered freely by God when we honestly recognize our distance from God and the marks we have missed, and our relationship with God is restored and even enhanced.

I'm committed to the Wesleyan Quadrilateral, the method John Wesley outlined for ethical and theological reflection on issues of living: a reliance on Scripture, interpreted carefully in its historical context; Tradition, the wisdom of the sweep of Christian thought, theology, and practice; Reason, using the powers of reasoning to puzzle out all areas of human life, including scientific study and theological reflection; Experience, especially the experience of Christian believers in their journeys of faith.

I'm also committed to the Wesleyan Way of personal and social "holiness," a lifestyle of reflection, study, prayer, and meditation personally and expressed in action to improve the conditions of life for all people, societies, and the earth itself.

These factors lead me to be involved in the struggle for understanding and fully integrating those who are Lesbian, Gay, Bisexual, Transgender, Queer,* Intersex, and Asexual into the life of the church, especially The United Methodist Church. I think that the UMC and particularly the "Traditionalists" and some other conservatives have ignored or dismissed the science of sexuality, sexual differentiation, gender, and orientation, as well as the Christian Experience of LGBTQIA believers. In addition, the "traditional" view of same-gender sexual behavior appears to be based on a literalistic reading of faulty translations of specific words, especially in the English Bible. Details of this problem are amply addressed in this bibliography. JBenjaminRoe.com/quadbib.html

See my bibliography based on the Wesleyan Quadrilateral for sources for some of my commitments in the area of sexuality, sexual differentiation, sexual orientation, gender.

So in summary, yes, I have a point of view and will say it to whomever will listen!

"Queer" was a pejorative epithet reclaimed by activists to cover a wide spectrum of non-heterosexual cis-gender folk. See this article (one of many). wikipedia.org/wiki/Queer

—Ben Roe

Appendix E: Phyllis Carol Roe: Wounded Healer

A Remembrance by Ben Roe at the Memorial Service for Phyllis, at First United Methodist Church, Honolulu, 2001

Who was Phyllis Carol Roe? She was our sister, our friend, confidant, counselor, colleague, inspiration...

What was her essence, her spirit? Many words probably come to mind: free spirit; one who chuckled; one who listened carefully and said insightful one-liners; healer.

She was an influential presence among us. She touched many, many people in many ways. Her leadership touched and helped shape the AAPC, the Western Region, the Samaritan Center movement, and most especially the Samaritan Counseling Center of Hawai'i.

Where did her gifts come from? Where did she get her ability to be a "non-anxious presence," to "treat everyone as family"?

Henri Nouwen's image of the Wounded Healer is one particularly helpful way to understand Phyllis, it seems to me. She had a number of wounding experiences in her life and I think each one was transformed into something healing.

I was a source of wounding for her. The most literal wounds were those I made when she was in her first year, when I would bite her, according to my mother. Now that is taking sibling rivalry a bit too far, and I'm embarrassed to admit I did that! Perhaps part of her gentleness grew out of this experience...

She was just under one year old when I came down with polio. I don't know how much of my pain and trauma she witnessed before I disappeared into hospitals for three months, but she knew at some level how severe this illness was. Witnessing these kinds of things can change one. Even though I think she was born compassionate, I think this experience deepened her instinct for compassion.

But the deepest wound I think came years later, after we had separated for our respective seminaries, hers in New York City, mine in Claremont, California. My individuation was messy, drawn out and painful. One therapist has reminded me that there is no graceful way to individuate from what has been called an enmeshed family system. Through her experiences with our family, she developed a sense of the value of family, and she broadened it to include the world.

Death was a wounding experience: first her closest friend in college died in a car accident; then while she was in Atlanta, our sister Rebecca died of a ruptured aortic aneurysm after a long and difficult period of living with systemic lupus; our father Joe died also of a ruptured aortic aneurysm in the year before she and Michael came to the Islands; and her husband Michael himself died suddenly!

Any one of these experiences of death could have turned her against God permanently. Some of you know better than I the struggles associated with these experiences of death. As she worked through each of these painful wounding experiences, she grew more able to be present with others who were dealing with grief. She was able to stay with grieving individuals through the agony of loss and facilitate the healing process. She was able to be with them in the depths because she'd been there, knew the territory and knew that living again was possible.

Facing the certainty of her own early death and the uncertainty of its timing was also a wound. She lived for 7 years with the awareness that death could happen to her suddenly at any moment, without much warning. Her experience with a dissected aorta and aortic aneurysm, as well as her experience with our sister Rebecca's lupus, gave her a sensitivity for chronic conditions and a willingness to be a non-anxious presence with those who lived with these kinds of situations without running from them.

She once wrote that "having such an illness is like being in a crucible in which all of our usual denial is burned away, and we are left face to face with basic questions of life and death--and their meaning." She affirmed the "characteristically human" search for meaning, but said, "Perhaps the meaning lies, however, not in the cause of the disease, but in how we respond to it, in how we use the experience to learn and grow." She affirmed the possibilities of growth through facing death: "In looking death in the face we find the beauty in life. We also discover that in life and in death we are embraced and strengthened by the All Compassionate One who will never leave us." But we have to look. In a sermon on perspective, she quoted Elizabeth Barrett Browning: "Earth's crammed with heaven. Each common bush aflame with God. Yet only he who sees takes off his shoes. The rest set around and pluck blackberries."

She wrote once about Rebecca, "Was Rebecca healed? Beyond any doubt, yes she was healed. Was her disease cured? No. Did her faith make her whole? Rebecca would tell you that it was her faith in God through Jesus Christ that gave her the inner strength to face death and to live life. She came through her illness to believe in her worth as a person, to experience being loved and loving, and to know joy in simply living for one more day. Yes, by the grace of God Rebecca became whole as her body crumbled. I know because she was my sister."

My sister Phyllis could sit and listen intently and not say anything, being fully present, being a non-anxious presence, because she had allowed her wounds to be transformed into healing gifts. My wish is that we can work to or be open to allowing all our wounds, mistakes, and failures be transformed into healing gifts.

From JBenjaminRoe.com tribute to Phyllis, delivered July 14, 2001 at First UMC, Honolulu.

Acknowledgments and Gratitudes

I want to thank my wonderful life partner, "best friend forever" of over 55 years, Maggie, for taking a chance on me, for sharing herself and honoring my sharing. I say much more about our relationship in the chapter on Friendship, Love, and Marriage.

I'm grateful for my parents, Joe and Enid, for their faith commitments, their care for me, and for documenting my early life in a "Baby Book" and numerous photographs. These have been an important part of my journey of discovery.

Thanks to those who read early drafts of this book and gave helpful suggestions and raised good questions that led to deeper understandings and clarity of presentation, especially Maggie, Jill Eelkema, Cynthia Tuell, Amy Gearhart, Karla Stromberger, Harvey Martz, Steve Nixon, Marny Eulberg, and my sister Deb. I especially thank my editor, Erin Althaus and my publisher, Mindy Reed. I took almost all of their editing suggestions! Any errors which remain are entirely mine, most of them intentional.

To the therapists and counselors, some of whom are now deceased, who have helped me uncover, understand, clarify, work through, reframe, and choose better ways to think, to talk, to live, and to choose: thank you, thank you, thank you! You have helped me use my learning and healing to help others who want it. Especially Carlton Paine, Ph.D., psychologist and careful listener of Lincoln, Nebraska; Fred Walz, pastoral counselor, Denver; Larry Graham, professor of pastoral counseling at Iliff School of Theology; Mary Ann Van Buskirk, pastoral counselor, Denver; and our marriage counselors Frank Kimper, a pastoral counseling professor at Claremont School of Theology, and Ellie Hites and Les Collins in Omaha. The supervisors I had when I was doing pastoral counseling myself helped me understand my clients, my responses, my theoretical perspective, and my practice of providing counseling.

I give thanks, too, for the medical care I've gotten over these many years, even those first hospitals that kept me alive and got me started on my rehabilitation journey. I value the care from the physicians, surgeons, and physical therapists over the years whose knowledge and care not only kept me alive but helped me have the quality of life I have enjoyed.

To my many friends and acquaintances over the years, I give thanks for the companionship, friendship, and reflections on life, faith, theology, justice, and technology—and for my failures of friendship, including my lack of consistent contact, I'm sorry. I hope what you learn about me in this piece will give you some understanding and hopefully some compassion towards me and these failings.

About the Author

Ben was the first child and only boy of Methodist minister family Joe and Enid Roe. He had polio at two years five months, and after three orthopedic surgeries had a good recovery for 43 years or so. When the late effects of polio became prominent, he got his first three-wheel scooter around 1992, then a wheelchair in 2021. He has been a United Methodist minister, sexuality educator, pastoral counselor, and communications staffer at a regional denominational office. In addition, he has been an executive secretary, and a trainer, programmer and customer support for a Unix-based data acquisition system and an amateur radio operator. He has been a writer and an editor for several church publications. He has worked for inclusion of LGBTQIA persons in the United Methodist Church since 1978. He has come to see gender and sexual orientation as non-binary continua, with all kinds of gradations, complications, and complexities, and celebrates his attractions to persons regardless of their gender. He and his partner Maggie have been together for over 56 years, many of those involved in sexuality education and advocacy activities. He holds B.A. and Doctor of Ministry (D.Min.) degrees and an Instructor in Human Sexuality certificate.

www.ingramcontent.com/pod-product-compliance
Lightning Source LLC
LaVergne TN
LVHW020418070526
838199LV00055B/3656